Empath Healing Secrets

By

Theo Franklin

Text Copyright © Theo Franklin

All rights reserved. No part of this guide may be reproduced in any form without permission in writing from the publisher except in the case of brief quotations embodied in critical articles or reviews.

Legal & Disclaimer

The information contained in this book and its contents is not designed to replace or take the place of any form of medical or professional advice; and is not meant to replace the need for independent medical, financial, legal or other professional advice or services, as may be required. The content and information in this book have been provided for educational and entertainment purposes only.

The content and information contained in this book have been compiled from sources deemed reliable, and it is accurate to the best of the Author's knowledge, information, and belief. However, the Author cannot guarantee its accuracy and validity and cannot be held liable for any errors and/or omissions. Further, changes are periodically made to this book as and when needed. Where appropriate and/or necessary, you must consult a professional (including but not limited to your doctor, attorney, financial advisor or such other professional advisor) before using any of the suggested remedies, techniques, or information in this book.

Upon using the contents and information contained in this book, you agree to hold harmless the Author from and against any damages, costs, and expenses, including any legal fees potentially resulting from the application of any of the information provided by this book. This disclaimer applies to any loss, damages or injury caused by the use and application, whether directly or indirectly, of any advice or information presented, whether for breach of contract, tort, negligence, personal injury, criminal intent, or under any other cause of action.

You agree to accept all risks of using the information presented inside this book.

You agree that by continuing to read this book, where appropriate and/or necessary, you shall consult a professional (including but not limited to your doctor, attorney, or financial advisor or such other advisor as needed) before using any of the suggested remedies, techniques, or information in this book.

Contents

Introduction 1

Chapter 1: The Psychology of Empathy 5

1.1 What is Empathy?... 5

1.2 Age and Empathy Development....................10

1.3 Role of Empathy 21

1.4 Empathy: A basic trait......................................24

1.5 What Causes People's Lack of Empathy.......27

   1.5.1 Things that people who are not empathetic don't do..28

   1.5.2 Disorders associated with people who lack empathy 30

   1.5.3 Dealing with people who lack empathy 32

1.6 Empathy vs. Sympathy 38

1.7 Are You an Empath or Just Highly Empathetic? 42

Chapter 2: What is an Empath?........................52

2.1 What to expect as an empath, the day to day life 57

Chapter 3: Becoming Self- Aware.....................62

3.1 How to Improve Self-Awareness 65

Chapter 4: Developing Your Empathic Abilities . 69

4.1 Turning Empathy into Your Strength 75

Chapter 5: Common Dangers in the Life of an Empath 87

Chapter 6: Overcoming Your Fears 93

Chapter 7: Protecting Yourself as an Empath – Setting Boundaries 109

7.1 The Relationship between an Empath and Narcissist 121

7.1.1 Different Types of Narcissists Every Empath Should Look Out For 125

7.1.2 How to Deal with Narcissists 130

Chapter 8: Dealing with Exhaustion and Fatigue 133

Chapter 9: Adapting to the Real World 147

9.1 How to Apply Empathy in Your Everyday Life 149

9.2 How to Apply Empathy in Your Romantic Relationship 152

9.3 How to Apply Empathy at Workplace 154

Conclusion 158

Introduction

I always knew that I was very intuitive, but because I wanted to fit in, I tried to shut those gifts off from an early age. But, the more I listened to my emotions, the more I felt I need to use that gift.

I always knew I was different as a little kid. I was not one of the kids you could see playing outside all the time. Although I participated in most things that other children did, they were generally inside. I knew I had a connection with all types of people. Previously, I thought it was normal, and everyone experiences it. I connected not only with my family and friends' mind, but also with strangers'. I could easily tap into the feelings they are experiencing and strike a sense of deep bonding and communication that most people could only dream of.

You probably think that I fit the description of a "people's person," but the truth is, I don't. I am not even close to that term. Having this "ability" is not always fun, but I will say having this trait has been helpful to me growing up, especially in a city environment that can be pretty challenging.

For example, I have talked my way out of bullies bashing my friends and have befriended a lot of junkyard dogs that used to scare me. I have had total strangers tell me the most intimate information about them. I did not make enemies, and even my ex-partners are still my good friends. You would think this ability would've taken me to the upper levels of society, but it didn't.

When I was younger, it was cool and flattering to have people ask me for advice or just be an ear to help them, but eventually, I started noticing something. People's problems, struggles, apprehensions, and other negative feelings affected me. Don't get me wrong. I didn't mind helping people. In fact, I enjoyed it. The only problem was that the more I felt their emotions, the more it ate me up. I felt like an emotional dumping ground for other people. This gave me a high level of anxiety, and of course, as a teen, a lot of self-medicating ensued.

The first time I heard the word empath was almost 3 years ago from my life coach. She mentioned that she was an empath. I asked what it meant. She said, "It means I am capable of reading and understanding emotions." "So, you are a person who has empathy?" I asked again. "No. It's more than just someone who has empathy," she responded.

She then started explaining it further the best she could, and it got me wondering if I was also an empath.

I could relate when she said that it had to do with knowing what people were really feeling, distancing from her body in order to cope, and searching relief in the metaphysical world.

I learned I was an empath all along.

I learned how this was a gift that not everyone had, and so, it deserved to be cherished. I admitted that it was not easy. In fact, it could be hard sometimes, but I learned to live with it and make the most of it.

If there's something I regret about this whole thing, however, it is that I wish I was aware of it earlier. I wish I knew how to deal with this ability, and I could have saved myself from hours and hours of sessions with my psychiatrist talking about my mental health.

This is something I don't want you to go through.

So, in this book, I will give you a sneak peek into the life of an empath, how to live with this innate ability, how to overcome the common struggles and everything else you need to know in order to live a happy, content life as an empathetic person.

Chapter 1

The Psychology of Empathy

1.1 What is Empathy?

You can consider empathy as an emotional trait, and the best way to understand empathy is to know how to recognize it. In order to help you recognize empathy better, let me give some examples of empathy from real life.

Empathy is the foundation of social skills. Generally speaking, it is your ability to see yourself in someone else's situation. Many use this term in different ways, and it could be broken down into two categories: emotional empathy and cognitive empathy.

- ❖ **Emotional empathy** is when a person can pick up the emotions of other people and have a suitable feeling in response. For example, if they are around someone who is close to them getting news that upsets them, they might feel sympathetic or sad on their behalf. Similarly, if the person who is close to them receives good news, they feel happiness and excitement. Sometimes, people think that empathy is simply an ability to feel what another person is experiencing. On the other hand, some people recognize it as empathy when one acts on those feelings and shows support, worry, or other such feelings.

- ❖ **Cognitive empathy** is one's ability to more logically get inside the head of someone and adopt their perspective. This doesn't necessarily involve feeling what the person is feeling. However, you are rationally aware of how they are feeling. Once again, there are people who see this form of empathy as just being able to assume what's going through a person's head, while others do not think someone is empathetic unless they express it through actions or words.

It doesn't take much effort to see how these skills could be useful in social situations. A few examples are stated below:

- Whether they are feeling happy or anxious, you are able to show someone that you are aware and concerned about what they are currently going through.
- While having a conversation with someone, you are able to bring up topics people will likely be interested in and avoid the ones that may bother or offend them.
- You could generally have a great sense of what people would like to get out of an interaction, and give it to them accordingly (e.g., do they want to talk about themselves or emotions, or do they want you to ask about something they want to talk about but don't know how to initiate it?)
- You could simply adjust the style of your conversation, depending on the person's character, sense of humor, etc.
- You know when to be extra supportive of people. For example, they are going to have a presentation; you tell them that you believe that they will perform well.
- When having a disagreement or negotiation with someone, you try to see things from their

point of view, instead of blindly thinking you are the one who's right and whatever they say is meant to attack you.

❖ You'll normally approach people with an open mind, accepting their attitude – whatever it may be.

Having empathy does not mean you need to please people, always base your actions on other people's feelings, and only say what people want to hear. Empathy is what gives you a cue on how to react to certain situations – to avoid hurting people. For example, if you have to give someone criticism, you can tell the truth, even if it hurts, without making them feel that you are attacking them.

Empathy is an important part of one's emotions and is itself a particular emotion which involves a feeling element of connection and a physical reaction of both verbal and nonverbal communication. Generally, empathy is when you feel what another person is feeling as if you are the one in their situation. Empathy generates emotional connection and involvement, and this could be with friends, lovers, family members, and even strangers. Empathy relates to connectedness and a feeling of simply knowing what another person is going through. There are people that are just more empathetic than others while at the same time, there are also some people who may find it hard to have empathy.

Empathy is closely related to intuition. This is in a way how intuition helps a person understand and recognize other people's emotions. Even though emotions are concealed and not demonstrated, empathy can help identify these emotions through instinct. Empathy is, therefore, seen as recognizing other individuals' emotions through perception and is marked by a feeling of having a connection with the other person.

In any form of leadership situation like in social leadership and political leadership, it's important for leaders to feel a certain level of empathy with every member of the group as the leaders have to feel connected to the groups to make an impression in their decisions and opinions. Professionals like teachers also must feel empathy with the students as this generates a connectedness without which the teaching experience is meaningless for the teachers and students alike. Empathy has something to do with motivating or influencing another person by tapping in on his feelings or emotions. It's much easier to impact or change others if you're keenly aware of what they're thinking or feeling since this helps to predict the possible responses.

1.2 Age and Empathy Development

Building a Foundation

A 2-month-old girl, Sarah, starts being fussy when her mom, Susan, puts her in the car seat. Susan tries to soothe her by talking to her, but it just makes her fussing worse. She starts rubbing her tummy, but she just kept on crying. She then decided to pick her up, put her on her shoulder, and slowly rocks her – that's when she starts to calm down. Even though Susan responds rapidly to the discomfort Sarah was experiencing, she performed a gradual process. By her gradual approach, she's letting her assist in her own consoling. The job of the newborn child is to learn, with care, how to soothe herself. Just like how talking to a baby helps them learn how to talk, soothing a baby helps them how to comfort themselves, and eventually, apply these traits to others.

Throughout these development interactions, the baby falls deeply in love with those they see all the time and treat them with care and show them their love. These powerfully-felt connections provide them with the emotional capability for feelings of empathy. Empathy, an essential element of emotional and social development, arises within steady and caring relationships throughout the years. Much of the basis is laid throughout early attachments developed in childhood.

Imitating Emotions

At 10 months, Charles loves wearing any adult shoes he sees and showing it off to adults around him for approval. He's starting to learn how to read facial expressions and gestural cues, doing things over and over again that make people smile. He's starting to be more mindful of other people as well as what they feel — an essential forerunner to feel empathy.

While a lot of little infants are sensitive when it comes to people's emotions, they are yet to fully grasp the feeling of empathy. Julie, for instance, starts to cry when she notices that her mother is not around. Luke, same as her age playing next to her, all of a sudden turns somber. Julie's anxiety has prompted the same emotion in Luke. Even though he has been affected by Julie's tears, he isn't yet aware of why she is crying.

Toddlers perceive and imitate the adults who they interact with on a regular basis. When the 3-year-old Mary falls and scrapes her knee at school, her classmates gather around her and watch as their teacher helps and comforts her. The teacher's action will be used as an example by kids for comforting others when the same things happen again in the future. Empathetic behavior has to be modeled repeatedly by adults and stimulated in children before this trait becomes a natural part of them.

Early Signs of Empathy

As discussed earlier, developing empathy is a gradual process. At first, a kid might only have a tad bit impression that there's something wrong going on.

At about 1-year-old, children begin "social referencing" – observing things they see the adults do. They learn that facial expressions represent different emotions and feelings. Before they turn 2 years old, children show the ultimate ancestor to empathy – learning that other people can have different feelings and emotions from them. In a study performed on a group of 18-month-olds, this conclusion was drawn. The toddlers were offered either broccoli or crackers – and most of them chose crackers. They were then set up with a group of adults who were instructed to make "yummy" face when they see the broccoli or "yucky" face when they see the crackers. The result: The toddlers were offering them the broccoli even though they chose the crackers themselves.

However, while toddlers start to read facial impressions, it's still hard work for a two-year-old to fully understand other people's perspective. When you try to tell them you are too tired to play or you don't have enough money to buy something they want, they are still likely to insist you do the thing they want. Their strong desire for something will easily offset any empathic feelings they might have.

What You Can Do

- ❖ Tell them what others feel: "Mike is sad because he spilled his drink on the floor." This will help the children to be more aware of their own feelings as well as the others.
- ❖ Gently guide the children's actions to inspire empathy: "Look at that dog, he seems so hungry. Let's give them some food to eat and something to drink!"

3 to 4: An Awareness of Feelings

At the age of 3 to 4 years, as any parent knows, children are not at their most selfless and generous behavior. They aren't developmentally capable of fully grasping the idea behind empathy. However, this does not mean you should not keep teaching it to them. If you see them hit their sibling or hurt an animal, for example, you can say, "That's not a very nice thing to do. Imagine it was you who has been hurt or treated like that. Wouldn't it hurt?" At some point, your words may effectively kick in, although it may take a while.

Lessons in Sincerity

Social psychologists believe that even though we are born with a capability for empathy, people could also learn to be empathic. However, empathy needs to be spontaneous, natural, and genuine. If you force a toddler to say sorry to someone without explaining why or how their action relates to other people's feelings, they are not really displaying or learning the act of empathy. Actually, the insincerity of this manner may even teach them other people's feelings really don't matter. Instead, if your kid hurts someone, you can explain how their action made someone feel, and that it's not alright. Then that's when you need to ask them what they can do to make them feel better – to ask for a sincere apology.

A Different Perspective

There are three-year-olds who may not be capable of responding to another person's feelings if they do not share the same thoughts and feelings toward the same situation.

Perception has a lot to do with empathy. By preschool age, children start to understand different kinds of emotions pretty well and start to understand that everyone is going through different emotions. However, children have to know that not all possible reactions to feelings are okay. Sometimes, children laugh at others only because everyone else around them does or as a reaction to being happy that it did not happen to them. When Joan falls in the slippery mud, kids around her would laugh and think it was funny. But a 4-year-old Ronnie is sensitive to what his friend is feeling, helping her get up instead of laughing at her.

What You Can Do

Here are some means in which you can help young people to learn how to be more empathic and appreciative toward things and the feelings of people around them:

- ❖ Teach your kids words related to feelings and emotions. Together, make faces in a mirror and show them what facial expressions they can make based on particular emotions – when they are happy, scared, angry, sad, etc.

- ❖ Show them pictures portraying different emotions and empathic situations. You can use a camera to take pictures of thoughtful interactions within the community and then label the pictures with descriptions of the good deeds.
- ❖ Keep the conversation open. Always ask them what would make him feel better when you see them distressed and try to come up with solutions.
- ❖ Ask flexible questions that will encourage empathy. One of the questions you can ask is, "What do you think we can do to make your sister feel better?" Your child will then brainstorm expressive ways to demonstrate kindness.
- ❖ Always be a kind and empathic role model. Show nonverbal and verbal approaches while working with the needs of your children. Initiate kind gestures like hugs, patting, and rubbing. Always use a soft, calming voice to avoid intimidating them.

5 to 6: Showing Compassion

Kids do not have the cognitive skills to completely understand the idea of empathy until they reach the age of 8 or 9. But at the age of 5 to 6 years old, they might already be preoccupied with fair-mindedness and are worried about being treated nicely, and they want those who are close to them to also be treated nicely. To develop this trait, there are some things you can do.

Talk Through Discomfort

Children this age are sometimes cautious every time they encounter people who act, look, or sound differently from anyone they are familiar with. And young kids sometimes say something or ask questions that parents may find awkward or even embarrassing, like "Why does he look like that?" referring to people with disability.

When this happens, you don't have to be hard on your kids. After all, they just shared their reactions, and they didn't know how it will affect others. Instead, listen benevolently and answer their questions as well as what's wrong with the way they asked it. Keep in mind that the best way to ease children's fears is to engage in a very normal way. In other words, kids take their cues from the reactions they get from adults.

Encourage Their Kind Instincts

You can use evocative praise whenever you see your child approaching someone else with compassion. This encourages their desire to do compassionate things. You can use sentences like these:

- ❖ "Thank you for bringing me a glass of water when I got back from the gym last night. It really made me feel better."
- ❖ "Your grandma loved the letter you wrote to her on Christmas; she said it was the best gift she received in the whole year."

Discussing Feelings

Empathy develops from self-awareness. As your 5 or 6 years olds become more conscious of their own emotions, they start to identify them in others, and their emotional vocabulary develops. With this improved language ability, the doors open to thorough discussions regarding emotions that are the main way for developing empathic skills. These discussions may come from a current event, a classroom situation, a photograph, or a TV show that provokes an emotional response.

Fascinatingly, children at this age like talking about themselves. And when you take time to talk about the emotions of a book character, for example, or the feelings of someone's feeling after an argument, you give children the raw materials for having compassionate understandings and actions.

Reading Cues

Empathy needs the nonverbal skill of observation. Kids at this age are learning how to "read" others' feelings based on their gestures, actions, words, as well as facial expressions. When you talk to kids at this age, they are likely to look at your face as if they are scanning you for a hint to the feelings behind every word you say. Use this is an opportunity to develop their empathy.

The capability to read nonverbal cues plays a big part in the development of the social skills necessary for regular interaction. At circle time, the kids are in a predominantly high-spirited mood, wiggling and giggling as the teacher smiles and moves with them. Noticing the time, the teacher shifts her movements to prepare for a story, and her facial expression turns more serious and focused. Just like silent magic, some children notice her shift and calm down.

Those who are capable of watching, listening, and observing the emotions and actions of people around them are usually the ones who turn to be more successful in life. A conscious arrangement of self with others begins with the development of empathy during the early years. If you are able to show empathy, your kids will likely follow.

1.3 Role of Empathy

In general, the definition of empathy is one's ability to sense the emotions of others, along with the ability to make a judgment on what someone else might be thinking. In common jargon, empathy is usually defined by the metaphors: seeing through someone else's eyes and standing in someone else's shoes.

Psychologically speaking, there are essentially four different types of empathy us, humans have, namely self-empathy, cognitive empathy, emotional empathy, and compassionate empathy. Now, let's talk about each of them.

• **Self-empathy** - Self-empathy is when we feel empathy towards ourselves, being aware of our own feelings and dissatisfactions with understanding and compassion. While this doesn't make any problems go away, or magically turn things around, it definitely helps you feel connected with your own self. It is also an effective tool to express yourself with more honesty and makes dealing with problems more endurable.

• **Emotional empathy** - It means having the same feelings physically along with the other person as if their emotions are contagious. It makes one well-attuned to other people's feelings, which is an advantage in day to day dealings. There is a disadvantage associated with emotional empathy that happens when people do not have the ability to manage their own emotions. This can be viewed as psychological exhaustion leading to burnout as commonly seen in professionals. The purposeful detachment cultivated by those in the medical profession is a way to avoid burnout. But when the detachment leads to indifference, it can seriously impact the quality of professional care.

• **Cognitive empathy** - It means being aware of what another person feels and what is going through their mind. It's extremely useful when it comes to negotiations or motivating someone. It is believed that those who have good cognitive empathy can make great leaders as they tend to have an ability to move people and help them give their best on whatever they do. This type of empathy, however, comes with a disadvantage. Too much of cognitive empathy can make them exploit others to the point where it makes them uncomfortable. Such people tend not to have sympathy for their victims, and they expertly use their ability to manipulate people.

• **Compassionate empathy** – Also called as empathic concern, this form of empathy does not simply mean being aware of someone else's predicament and feel with them but instinctively help them as well, if necessary. Actually, compassionate empathy is the most important ingredient of an empathic response in a certain situation. It's the type of empathy that is most useful for those who work as social volunteers.

1.4 Empathy: A basic trait

Empathy is integrally present in humans at different levels and, so, we are affected by others' predicament in different ways. Females usually score higher on standard tests of empathy, emotion recognition, and social sensitivity, in comparison to males.

The presence of empathy as an inherent quality in all of us can be established by the way a child responds to the emotions of people around him. Aside from children, even animals have their own ways of expressing their worries or concerns when their members or their owners are feeling distressed. They would move around and touch their body on other animals or humans to show empathy. Aside from humans, a lot of other creatures show the presence of empathy to a different extent.

A cruel yet fascinating proof for the presence of empathy in animals came from research performed in 1964 by the American Journal of Psychiatry. The study shows rhesus monkeys denied pulling a chain that sent food to themselves because if they did so, it would give their companion a shock. One monkey stopped pulling the chain for more than 10 days after seeing another monkey getting a shock. Those monkeys literally starved themselves in order to avoid hurting other animals.

Empathy plays a big part in almost every aspect of our lives. While empathy is usually inherited, it could definitely be cultivated. The role of empathy in the life of a person actually depends on its conceptualization by the individual, which differs extensively. Nevertheless, empathy acts to replicate what has been observed and makes a helpful or settling atmosphere.

Empathy is an effective communication skill that's actually underused by a lot of people. It lets you understand thoughts and ensuing feelings generated by them in others. Empathy also helps a person to respond to other people's feelings compassionately so that they could win their trust, which stimulates communication further.

Empathy is beyond sympathy, which makes the person understand others with sensitivity and compassion. That's why it's very important to apply this trait in the workplace, where a lot of people work together in order to achieve a certain goal. It helps ensure great respect for the co-workers, thus nurturing a pleasant atmosphere in the place of work.

In the same way, empathy is useful in our professional life because aside from easing communication, it helps us be a sympathetic listener to our clients, which means we can understand them better.

Since empathy helps us communicate better and listen sympathetically, we stand a great chance of making our social and personal relationships successful. Actually, empathy can nurture all kinds of relationships we get into or are currently in.

It's pretty obvious how empathy affects our lives with far-reaching results. We must help our children to develop this trait as it is seen as highly beneficial in many aspects of life. Because empathy stimulates pro-social behavior, it is going to help our children generate close relationships, keep friendships, and cultivate better communities.

1.5 What Causes People's Lack of Empathy

There are people in our life who add shine to it, while there are others that darken our path and make it hard to navigate. Correspondingly, there are the ones who would do great things to help us and others who would rather not move a finger even if we asked. The latter is a good indication of lacking empathy.

There are relationships that develop our path while there are others that don't. Do you ever wonder why there are some people who can't accept that other people can commit a mistake and they are sorry? Have you ever seen someone who does something bad to others without remorse? These people are not likely to have empathy. There is a big chance that as long as it doesn't happen to them, they don't care.

As you know by now, empathy is one's ability to understand another person's reality and being aware of what they may feel. But not everyone has this quality.

In this chapter, let's talk about what these people are like and what disorders are related to the incapability to feel empathy. We're also going to discuss how we can relate to people who lack this ability.

The less empathetic you are, the fewer friends you'll have. Put yourself in other person's shoes to help yourself grow and allow your relationships to improve.

1.5.1 Things that people who are not empathetic don't do

People who care nothing about others don't have the capacity to understand or recognize how another person might be feeling. So, here are things people without empathy don't usually do.

Worry about others. If they are not paying attention to you, then it's maybe because they are too focused on themselves or because they simply don't care about you.

They are not sensitive. Even though you tell them about what you are thinking and feeling, they usually don't show interest in understanding what you are saying.

They don't trust others. By not understanding what other people may think and feel, they tend not to trust anyone but themselves.

They don't show compassion. For them, it's not their responsibility to relieve other people's pain or suffering.

With these traits in mind, it might be easier for you to recognize which people around you are not empathetic. You have to remember, however, that seeing one of the characteristics mentioned above doesn't mean that a person doesn't have empathy. Of course, these traits may still root for different reasons.

Selfish people who lack empathy

People who lack empathy just find it hard to put themselves in another person's shoes. That's why it's quite easy for them to ignore others' thoughts, feelings, and desires. Selfishness is definitely one of the most common characteristics of a person who lacks empathy.

People who lack empathy tend to only think about their well-being first and disregard other people's well-being and interests. Furthermore, they may take advantage of other people and situations for their own benefit.

Furthermore, they tend to push the boundaries of reciprocity. This means they only choose to give if they know that they are going to get something in return. They don't do things neutrally. They might relate to us, but in almost an unfriendly way, trying to manipulate others as much as they can.

So, those who lack empathy can feel quite cold. When you experience an unpleasant encounter with them, you may end up feeling misunderstood or feel that they don't really care about it. This is for the reason that they find it hard to connect with others.

1.5.2 Disorders associated with people who lack empathy

All of us may show the aforementioned traits at times. However, there are some who have these traits on a regular basis. There are psychological disorders that are closely related to lacking empathy.

Narcissistic personality disorder. These people tend to be self-absorbed and only care about themselves.

Furthermore, they have no problem with leaving other people behind. The lack of empathy in this personality disorder is related to the fact that they cannot see beyond themselves.

Psychopathy. This disorder has to do about the incapability to adapt to social norms. Those who have this disorder find it difficult to connect to others.

Borderline personality disorder. Those who suffer from this disorder normally have emotional instability, which makes it hard for them to keep stable relationships. Understanding or predicting other people's emotions is a challenge for them.

If you make an effort to explain to these people how their actions may affect others negatively, they normally don't understand or just ignore your explanation and may even try to make you feel guilty by trying to turn it back on you, telling you that you were the problem in the first place. Be careful. A person who doesn't have empathy can cause a lot of pain for those who are very empathetic.

1.5.3 Dealing with people who lack empathy

Some of those who lack empathy not only having a hard time understanding us, but they can also manipulate others to get what they want. Here are some ways to deal with them.

Set boundaries. You choose how far these people can run you. Don't let them take advantage of you and take you for granted.

Choose the people in your life wisely. If people are starting to get toxic in your life, then learn how to let them go.

Be confident. Say what you want to say, and say it in the most assertive way. By doing this, you can effectively convey the message.

If you don't emotionally feel connected with someone, then leave. However, you still have to keep in mind that extremes will not lead you anywhere. It's so easy to commit the mistake of just caring only about our interests. This does not automatically mean that we have no empathy. Furthermore, what is important is to choose the people we spend our time with.

People who don't have empathy are truly disinterested in other people. It's very hard for them to put themselves in other people's shoes and understand how they may feel and see. Furthermore, they are almost apathetic about most things that are going on around them.

Avoid people who are trying to control your thoughts and making you feel guilty. They are simply trying to take you into a place where they can control you.

Coming across as cold and insensitive

One way people may seem socially awkward is when aspects of their empathy are not well developed, and they unintentionally come off as inconsiderate and obtuse.

Less developed emotional empathy

❖ Not being responsive when people feel happy or upset.

- ❖ Giving overturning, tone-deaf responses to those who are feeling distressed, e.g., "Why are you crying over that video of an animal dying? It's just an animal."
- ❖ Appearing uncaring by not showing a lot of reaction to bad news about others, e.g., looking untroubled when they heard someone got into an accident.

Less developed cognitive empathy or ability to consider the perspectives of others

- ❖ Talking about a topic that bores others as they have not thought, "Maybe they would not be interested in this topic."
- ❖ Carelessly offending others by making insensitive or edgy jokes with the wrong crowd.
- ❖ Dropping comments that involuntarily insult people as they did not think about what the people they are talking to would feel.
- ❖ Talking about topics that are unsuitable for your company, e.g., talking about your political or religious view without caring about their beliefs.

- Voicing opinions at unsuitable times, e.g., talking about how you disagree with gay marriage even if a gay person is within earshot.
- Being nastily blunt and nonchalantly critical, e.g., "Your clothes don't look good on you. You should lose weight."
- Paying no attention to things that are important to others, e.g., greeting someone on their special day, not caring about someone's milestone.
- Looking down on others for what they see as their bad decisions, without considering how their life circumstances have been totally different from theirs.
- Being impolite and difficult to service staff as they are at a lower position.
- Taking friends for granted by always making them do nice things without realizing they would like you to show the odd bit of gratitude in return.

Why people can come by as insensitive and unsympathetic

- ❖ They are socially inexpert and either believe it is not their responsibility that they must care about the feelings and thoughts of others, or they know, but they're just not too good at it. They might unconsciously have a mindset of, "I would not get hurt if it was me, so they shouldn't too."
- ❖ They have no clue how to express care or concern, or it's something that makes them feel agitated and awkward. They have no clue what to do when a friend feels bad. They might come off emotionally blank as they are too stuck in their head, worrying about how they have no idea how to react.
- ❖ They are usually more logical and detached, and hardly ever get as emotional about things. News that might be upsetting for some might mean nothing to them.
- ❖ People with a more distant liberated social style sometimes inadvertently become too absorbed with their own needs and forget to think about

others. It doesn't necessarily mean that they are selfish monsters. It just happens that they develop some bad habits, and sometimes, they have no control over it.

❖ This is not to say that all teenagers are spoiled or evil or anything, however, sometimes, empathy is not as important to younger people just because they have not had enough experience in life. They have not encountered enough suffering or been exposed to a lot of contrasting worldviews and so have a harder time understanding people who are hurting or who see things differently than they do. Again, they are not totally unsympathetic sociopaths. It's just that their empathetic responses are not well-developed yet.

❖ When it comes to cognitive empathy, people with Asperger's Syndrome usually have a hard time catching up on another person's perspective. In terms of emotional empathy, they may have a problem reading other people's non-verbal communication and discerning their feelings. If they do notice someone's emotions, they normally have no problem with having an emotionally empathetic response. However, they might have trouble gesturing that response if their facial expressions are on the blanker side.

❖ If someone is experiencing stress and emotional chaos, their condition will certainly narrow their center onto their own problems.

So far, we have discussed some more benign, accidental reasons someone may come off as insensitive. However, the fact is there are people who lack empathy because they have got a selfish, self-centered, conceited, or close-minded side to their personality. Those are obviously negative characters, which we may show every now and then. But if you believe that you do have them, know that it is always something you can change if you want.

1.6 Empathy vs. Sympathy

Aside from empath, another word that many people think is a synonym for empathy is sympathy. Sympathy is the understanding, perception, and reaction to the distress, agony, or need of another person. This can be considered as an empathic concern which is driven by a switch in perception, from a personal viewpoint to the perception of another person or group who is in need. Empathy and sympathy are usually used interchangeably. The main difference between the two is probably the fact that sympathy is an emotion, while empathy is a trait. This just goes to show that the two words not only have different meanings but also origins.

Sympathy is an emotion that you feel for another person. Unlike empathy, this doesn't make you feel directly. Instead, you may feel a negative emotion that generally encourages you to do something to help them. When a person is in misery or distress, a person who sympathizes may show his trouble with the situation in the form of words or other forms of expressions. Some words that you may hear from them are, "I'm sorry it happened," "This must be hard for you," or" If you want someone to talk to, I'm here for you."

But those are the things that an empath or empathetic person would say, too! So what's the difference?

Sympathy is not always great. It can be shallow and superficial. You might feel bad, yes, but you can also act like you care even if you don't. Sometimes, this emotion can also be deceitful. You can say sorry to someone all day and not mean it.

When something bad happens to you, your whole neighborhood may feel sympathetic. Even the people who you thought didn't like you may offer their sympathy. But deep down, they just want to do it for the sake of not looking like a bad person. They say sorry, but they would not even exert an effort to help you even if they could. Actually, some may even act like they are sorry for you, but deep down, they are laughing at what happened. Yes, this happens.

Here are some situations that highlight the differences between the two words.

Situation: "I broke my phone."

Sympathetic: "Oh, I'm so sorry about that."

Empathetic: "How did it happen? Let me see if I can help you fix it."

Situation: "My dog passed today."

Sympathetic: "Oh, no. That sucks. He was a good dog."

Empathetic: *Cries with you*

Situation: "I passed my exam today."

Sympathetic: "Oh, really? That's nice, congrats!"

Empathetic: "Oh, wow! I always knew you would pass! I'm very proud of you! Let's go out and celebrate!"

Again, empathy is when a situation makes you feel their pain and happiness, even if the situation did not happen to you directly. Empathy does not come with the negative connotation about the other person, whereas sympathy usually does. You may feel empathy for friend passing an exam, which means you will feel the same happiness he's feeling, the same way you empathize your friend whose heart is broken after a breakup; sometimes, you might even feel extreme emotion more than the person experiencing it. As you can see, empathy is beyond sympathy.

Empathetic personality is rare but still exists and definitely not a dying breed, but these people are a gift which makes the world a better place, for sure. It's definitely the only trait that joins you with the life current within, with other living creatures and things.

Empathy comes straight from the heart. It is a powerful trait that anyone who has it should embrace.

1.7 Are You an Empath or Just Highly Empathetic?

The main attribute of an empath is feeling and understanding other people's emotions due to their high sensitivity. These people face the world through their intuition and likely to have a hard time intellectualizing their emotions. So, as you can imagine, it's not always rainbows and butterflies for empaths all the time. When feeling overwhelmed with the effect of stressful emotions, empaths might have to deal with depression, panic attacks, food binge, chronic fatigue, and other emotion-related problems.

A lot of people are empathetic, but not a lot notice it. They may think that they're different in a deep way, but they can't directly identify what makes them different or entirely understand their emotional experiences. Being very empathetic means, it's easy for you to share and identify the emotions of another person as stepping in their shoes becomes automatic. What extremely empathetic people have in common is the ability to sense what other people think and feel.

It's important to find the difference between people who are very empathetic and those who are empaths. When your experiences and emotions cross over into being vague from your own, like you feel the physical and emotional pain of other people as if it is your own, you are probably an empath.

So, are you highly empathetic or not? Check out these eight signs and see if any of these are relevant to you.

1. You are highly sensitive

For empaths, it is very natural to be giving, good listeners, and spiritually open. In terms of having a big heart, empaths always win. Through thick and thin, these top-notch nurturers will surely be there for you all the time. But they could easily have their feelings hurt, as well; empaths are usually seen as too sensitive.

2. You can easily catch on the emotions of others

Empaths are well-adapted to the mood of other people, may it be good or bad. It's so easy for them to feel everything, and sometimes, it can be too extreme. They tend to be easily affected by negativity, like anxiety and anger, which could be very stressful for them. If they're surrounded by love and peace, however, their bodies take these on and make their overall mood flourish.

3. You are introverted

For most empaths, crowds can be overwhelming as this can intensify their empathy. Many empaths tend to be introverted and prefer one-on-one encounters or little groups. Even though an empath is more extraverted, they might choose to limit how much time they spend around crowded places like parties.

4. You are greatly intuitive

Empaths approach most things in their lives based on their intuition. It's necessary for them to develop their intuition and follow their gut feelings about others. This directs empaths to positive relationships and helps them avoid energy-sucking situations and people.

5. You constantly find yourself needing time alone

As super-responders, these people find being around with many people can be draining, so they occasionally need some time on their own to recharge their drained battery. Even a brief escape stops emotional burden. For instance, empaths would rather bring their own car when they attend a gathering, so it's easier for them to go home whenever they want.

6. You tend to become overwhelmed in intimate relationships

For many empaths, too much togetherness can be pretty challenging, so some of them tend to avoid intimate relationships. Deep down, they're afraid to be engulfed and to lose their identity. In order for empaths to be at ease throughout a relationship, the traditional example of being a couple should be redefined.

7. You are a target for energy vampires

The sensitivity of an empath makes them mostly easy prey for energy vampires, whose rage or fear can dry out their energy as well as their peace of mind. These vampires might not only drain the physical energy of an empath. Especially hazardous ones like narcissists can make empaths believe they are unlovable and unworthy. They also don't have time for toxic people who like dragging drama into their lives.

8. You get refilled in nature

The busyness of daily life could be excessive for an empath. But with the natural world, their energy can be restored and nourished. It helps them discharge their burdens, and they can take shelter in the wild green things or the ocean.

9. You have well-adjusted senses

The nerves of an empath can get worn by smells, noise, or excessive sounds.

10. You have a big heart and tend to give too much

Empaths are known to be some of the big-hearted people you will know, and it's so natural for them to relieve other people's pain. So, if you see them giving money to homeless people, helping a cat who got stuck at a tree, crying over disasters, then know that it's natural for them. They always go out of their way to help others as much as they could. They like making the problem of others as if it is theirs.

Did you find any of the points above relatable for you? As an empath, you can use a lot of these strategies to protect your sensitivities, like fiercely setting limits, time management, and boundaries with people that are draining you out. For some, being empathetic is a gift, but if not managed well, it could be destructive for you.

On the other hand, if you think that the signs mentioned above are too extreme, well, here are the signs that you could be just someone who is empathetic.

1. You are an amazing listener

People who are highly empathetic are a great listener. In fact, they would rather listen than speak as they want the other person to think that they care about them. In order to fully understand the problems or achievements that the other person is experiencing, they are interested to know every detail about what's going on in the other person's lives. They listen carefully to the words and also observe any non-verbal cues. They are also mindful, which means they are focusing their thoughts in the present moment and keeping engaged in the encounter.

2. You are a source of support and advice

Highly empathetic individuals who can naturally invest in the emotions of others can easily become a source of advice, guidance, and support for others — both professionally and personally. Their outstanding listening skills help them give out well-planned advice while making others feel understood, appreciated and loved. The combination of their listening skills and capability to share feelings makes them a great counselor. It's the reason why highly empathetic people gravitate to helping occupations, like teachers, therapists, and even medical practitioners.

3. You are a natural leader

Those who are highly empathetic can easily build trust with their employees, students, and others due to their natural capacity for honest interest in others compassion, and excellent listening skills. Leaders with high empathy are active listeners, which nurtures and promotes open communication due to the trust that this skill creates. When a principle of trust is established, any type of group flourishes.

4. You find big social settings draining

For highly empathetic people, big social situations can be very draining, just like how it is for empaths, introverts, and very sensitive people. Empathy mostly provokes both positive emotions as well as negative emotions that can rapidly make those with these abilities feel drained when overstimulated. Actually, based on a study from the University of Haifa in Israel, the social phobia has something to do with elevated sensitivity to the states of mind of other people.

5. You put the needs of others first

Those who are highly empathetic are persuaded to take care of others before thinking about themselves. They entirely put themselves in the shoes of the people or animals that are important to them; they put them first before their own needs. Because they're highly empathetic, they can make outstanding decisions regarding how their care affects others both emotionally and physically, without thinking about themselves.

6. You can detect the positive and the negative

The universe, including our body, is in a constant state of movement or vibration. For highly empathetic people, it's easy to naturally feel this energy and interpret emotions that surround them, may they be negative or positive. It's also easy for highly empathetic people to distinguish good vibes from bad vibes; although they might need additional input, like verbal cues and body language to successfully know them. For example, have you ever walked into a room and felt like there's something wrong? The atmosphere just feels so negative, and you felt so down.

7. You just love pets so much

Animals instinctively know when people like them. Pets are attracted to those who are highly empathetic and sensitive. Similarly, people who are highly empathetic can form strong relationships with their pets, sometimes more than humans. With that being said, people who have a great ability to understand animals' mental state can be labeled as "animal empaths."

Chapter 2

WHAT IS AN EMPATH?

Before reading this book, you probably thought that an "empath" is just the same with the word "empathetic" or "empathy." Well, they are sort of same, but not really.

So, what does it mean to be an "empath"? Does it mean you're a psychic or a too sensitive person? Are empaths usually the "good" type of people? Do they have natural gifts that are not seen in many people? And what do empaths do to make the most of the gifts to make a difference in the world or make an impact on people around them?

The truth is, it's very easy to describe what an empath is.

An empath is someone who has an extraordinarily strong sense of sensitivity and connection with the feelings and emotions of people around them. The word sensitive is probably the word that delivers the essence of what an empath is, better than any other word. But this is not to say that empaths are sensitive about their own feelings and emotions.

In other words, a lot of, not all, empaths are highly practical and pragmatic with their own emotions with a very strong personality. However, when it comes to other people's emotions, they get very sensitive.

So, does it mean that all empaths are naturally good people?

I'd say that this is a little tricky question, and there is no way that it can be answered with 100% certainty. BUT, I'm confident to say that empaths tend to be naturally caring, nurturing, and emotionally available people. And for them, it's always better to give than to receive.

What do empaths do that make them unique?

What they do is they "serve" those who are in need of them the most.

Okay, let me give you an example.

A lot of empaths have great intuitive gifts; this is mainly because they're far more naturally connected to the needs and emotions of those people around them. A lot of social scientists describe empaths as the ones who have a very REAL "sixth sense" due to their ability to identify, understand, and eventually bond with people and their situations in the way that a lot of others can't. This leads to an incredible amount of intuition and insight that can border on being unexplained.

Actually, there have been recent studies that suggest that the sixth sense that emotional empaths carry is pretty literally, a more highly developed brain in two specific parts.

The first part is the area in the brain that triggers a feeling of "connection" to others and the other part is located deep in the brain, which is believed to trigger synaesthesia, a not widely known but proven phenomena which allow people to hear colors and see sounds. It is also believed by many that there is a possible scientific explanation for everything -- From spirit communication to psychic abilities to sensing and seeing auras.

So, are all empaths psychic?

Definitely not, BUT there are many who are. And once you combine these two abilities, you get people who not just are unbelievably attuned to the energy released by others, but they can also see future events or future predictions.

A lot of the globally-known psychics and mediums may initially describe themselves as "empathic" because, for them, their natural gifts for sensing spirits and seeing what's going to happen in the future comes from their empathic abilities in the first place.

The reliance on external cues is probably the key difference between being an empath and empathetic.

The feeling of empathy takes an external trigger, such as receiving a phone call or scanning someone's face for his reactions. This is something an empath doesn't need.

What an empath needs to do is to consciously or subconsciously "look" at the energy of another person in order to know what he is going through. They don't need to be connected with them on a physical level in order to acquire that information.

It is an intuitive gift to be an empath, just like being a medium, and when used efficiently, they can have the capability to facilitate healing for living things around them.

But this gift is very rare.

Of course, some individuals are born "higher up" when it comes to the empath scale, just like how someone is better at singing than the others. But just like singing, along with other talents, the ability to be an empath can be developed. You have to make sure, however, that you open up to your trust and intuition that it's actually a gift, instead of some kind of freaky strange thing that has to be fixed as it makes you different from people around you.

Empathy, regardless of where you are on the scale, is absolutely amazing. Our empathy, whether it is derived from external cues or not, is what makes the connection between people. It generates trust, reverence, intimacy, compassion, and a sense of belonging. And more importantly, it expands our capability to hold space for one another to heal, transform, and grow.

2.1 What to expect as an empath, the day to day life

If you're one of the special people known as empaths, then you are likely to experience certain things in life that other people will not be able to understand.

Being an empath, you can experience things in life a bit differently compared to the rest of the world. You tend to feel the emotions coming from other people around you, and your heightened sensitivity lets you experience the suffering of others.

I, too, am an empath, so I completely understand many unusual challenges that highly empathetic people deal with a daily basis. I know how empaths are extremely prone to feeling overwhelmed by the stress of shouldering other people's emotions. Due to this, they're likely to go through things such as anxiety, panic attacks, depression, exhaustion, and as well as other symptoms that are not very easy to explain.

To a person who does not share the same heightened empathy as them, these things might not really make sense. Since empaths experience and feel so much, it is important for them to learn to manage some of the chaos for them to concentrate on themselves and their own lives. Being an empath might be quite a challenge, but it's not very hard to see it as a gift.

Here are the five common experiences an empath can relate to:

1. They FEEL Too Sensitive

It's common for an empath to feel too much, too much of what other people are going through, and too much of their own suffering. Empaths aren't too sensitive; they simply experience everything to a great extent since they're more emotionally developed compared to an average person. No wonder why they are considered amazing listeners, open-minded friends, and great at nurturing relationships.

2. They Can Absorb Emotions Too Quickly

Just like a sponge, an empath is going to absorb the emotions of people around him. Are you having a bad day? Well, then the empaths have it too. The moment they step into the room, they automatically adapt to the vibe around it. This is one of the main reasons why big crowds tend to drain them out.

Regardless of what emotions are going on around, even though you don't say anything to them, empaths can easily pick up on them. Negative emotions could have a great effect on an empath, and if they do not learn how to manage that kind of baggage, it can easily ruin their day.

3. They Have High Levels of Intuition

It's pretty easy for empaths to figure out when there is something wrong going on, or when someone is lying to their face. This is what we call the "gut feeling," but instincts are a very influential tool for empathic people. The moment they get a warning, they normally always listen to it. Fortunately, empaths tend to get surrounded by things and people that bring positive impact in their lives. Empaths tend to avoid people who they think are drama queens and toxic, although they have no problem helping them when they ask them for a hand.

4. They NEED Their Time Alone

Since empaths feel most of the things so strongly, and are very sensitive to the world around them, recharging their energy is definitely a must for them. Spending time alone is empaths' favorite way to find their inner-peace and recharge again. Doing so will help them get right back to their work as natural healers. The time they need may vary, it could be a few minutes, a few days, or even a couple of months. One of the unique traits of an empath is how they can make themselves feel like they are the most important in life for them, even though they love helping people and they make themselves available all the time, they can still make self-worth a priority.

5. They Love the Nature

Everyone needs time alone from time to time, and empaths are not an exception. For most of them, nature can have an amazing restorative effect on their life. They would like the idea of walking alone in the park, by the lake, on the beach, or hiking the mountain where they can just inhale the fresh air that helps them release the BSs in their lives. Honestly, this is something every person, whether an empath or not, should do at least once in a while. Life can truly be stressful and mentally draining, and spending proper time with nature can ease these negativities in our lives.

Not every person can easily relate to these experiences, and there's nothing wrong with that. Each person goes through life in their own unique ways. If ever you find yourself in the same situations mentioned above, make sure to pay attention to how you feel around others. Set your boundaries, and make a safe space for yourself for whenever you need it.

Chapter 3

BECOMING SELF- AWARE

Highly emphatic individuals normally lose the balance between their own emotions and others' because disconnecting themselves from others is something they are not good at. Normally, to offer a helping hand to others to "save the world," they tend to put themselves after the others, maybe at the expense of their own mental health and well-being. It's known that people who tend to prioritize other people's feelings more than their own needs usually experience depression or anxiety. It is normal that there are times we put someone else's feelings before ours, but this is something you should control before it destroys you.

Why Self-Awareness Is the First Step toward Empathy

In order for you to understand others better, we must first better understand ourselves. This is based on a new study published in the Journal of Cognitive Enhancement titled "Know Thy Selves: Learning to

Understand Oneself Increases the Ability to Understand Others."

For 3 months, psychologists collected data from 161 participants between the ages of 20 and 50 and had them take a course called contemplative training, which is derived from the Internal Family Systems model that teaches people that they're made up of different "sub-personalities," like your inner critic or happy voice.

The goal is that by being able to recognize the different parts of our personalities better, we're becoming more aware of our own patterns and tendencies, and this is able to help us navigate our relationships better and the way we connect with others.

The outcome of the study revealed that those who improved the most at seeing the different parts of their personality also improved at their capability to infer other people's mental states, a skill called the "theory of mind" or empathy.

So, this just goes to show that empathy and self-awareness are very closely related. When we become more aware of what really makes us who we are, it gets easier for us to distinguish the differences between ourselves and other people, and what makes them who they are.

As expected, both "empathy" and "self-awareness" are known to be the main basis of emotional intelligence. Technically, empathy is other-awareness, so it's literally the direct complement to self-awareness.

By definition, by becoming more aware of yourself, it also becomes easier for you to be aware of other people's feelings since the self/other contrast becomes clearer, and you start to define the ways you're both similar and different from others when it comes to thoughts and emotions.

That's an extremely important characteristic of empathy. It's not only about knowing the ways you're similar to other people but also knowing the ways you're very different from others.

It's impossible to show empathy to others if you think that everyone is the same as you are. That is not trying to understand another person's perspective; it is simply just projecting your own perspective onto other people.

For instance, I enjoy my time alone. I consider myself as introverted. However, I know that some people are not the same as me. I'm fully aware that not everyone is the same as me and that they don't enjoy staying alone as much as I do. Being aware of people's differences makes it easier for me to understand them, their emotions, and their actions. I just know that we have different personalities, and I should always keep that in mind whenever I spend time around them.

While that example is very simple, it surely shows how being able to recognize your own personality makes it easier for you to accept and manage the tendencies of others' direct relationship between empathy and self-awareness.

3.1 How to Improve Self-Awareness

So, what are the ways for you to improve your self-awareness? Here are four great ways you can start today to improve your self-awareness.

Meditation

Practicing meditation is definitely one of the best ways for anyone to improve their self-awareness. If you are a beginner, you can always start with simple exercises like the 100 breaths meditation, which is a good way to start becoming more aware of the internal world of feelings and thoughts and start accepting them in a non-judgmental way. Meditation is also going to also teach you how you can observe yourself and everything around without having to react to it, which is a great means of self-regulation.

Personality Quizzes

Being able to know more about your personality is also a great way to better understand how your mind truly works and how it can potentially affect others around you. It's easy to find free personality surveys on the internet that can help you have a better understanding of who you really are.

Contemplation

While meditation is going to teach you how to manage your feelings and thoughts, contemplation, on the other hand, is another essential aspect of analyzing your mind and learning more about how your mind works. Even simply taking 10 to 15 minutes to take a break and analyze your thought processes and beliefs can be an effective way to make yourself more aware of who you are.

Ask Others

Most of the time, our family and close friends can know more about us than we do, especially about certain characters that are very intensely ingrained in us that we usually take for granted. An essential way to develop self-awareness is to just ask a close friend. Ask them to describe you as a person. Ask them what they like about you and what they think you can change to make you a better person. Be creative and open-minded.

These are all smart ways to start developing and improving your self-awareness.

Is it possible for us to fully know ourselves? Well, that question is something that is not easy to answer. We are all unique and complicated human beings; so, it's more likely for us to not fully know ourselves.

But then again, actively building more self-awareness will surely help. And it would not simply help us improve ourselves but also improve your capability to empathize and connect with others in a genuine and expressive way. Always remember the importance of self-awareness, and try to do some of the exercises mentioned above to start your self-improvement.

Chapter 4

Developing Your Empathic Abilities

Empaths are known as intuitive individuals, more capable of reading people than reading "signs." Some empaths have those sorts of abilities, but you have to keep in mind that it's simply a small part of being a true empath.

Society's interest in the empathic person has just emerged recently after the work of the student of psychology, Jad Alexander. He started recognizing specific types of people that carried high and unique levels of sensitivity. These people were very intuitive, capable of sensing things that are unknown and something that cannot be seen in the majority of the world's population. After 30 years, his studies concluded that these people were in fact gifted, having the capacity to "know" things intuitively like when a person wanted them to call, when something's bugging in a person and would use some help, or even when someone is lost and need to know the right direction.

Jad came to the conclusion that these gifted individuals had unique alterations to their CNS or central nervous systems. The connection between the CNS and the brain was unique to the point that it made the thing we know as the "sixth sense," the sense that gets messages at a greater level than "ordinary" people and processes those messages in a unique way. This is a phenomenon that hasn't been evaluated by science yet, although there have been a lot of people that have invested resources and time into investigating what is an empath exactly once and for all.

With these studies, it has been revealed that people who are empathic have particular qualities. It's safe to say that the common denominator is the high level of sensitivity. Usually, these people are known as over-sensitive people, but maybe ultra-sensitive is the better term to use. They're very receptive to noise, smell, and light. Their sensory organs have a low threshold that amplifies the level to which their major senses react.

Along with these very light levels of sensitivity, empaths are often bombarded with a flow of random, irrational emotions and thoughts. The reason for this is that they usually "pick up" the feelings and thoughts of others, not only from people that are physically close to them but even of people who are miles and miles away from them. This is the psychic make-up of an empath, a "condition" that people who are not aware of their gift may find themselves struggling with. Due to the great amounts of information they're getting at the same time, and not having an idea about its nature, a lot of them are becoming overwhelmed and confused, usually turning to psychiatric experts to help them with their struggles.

Now, you might be wondering, how is an empath different from a psychic? Here is a simple explanation: a psychic SEES, while an empath FEELS.

The gut-feelings and hunches the empathic person experiences are essentially psychic messages. However, the problem is that these messages are delivered in the form of psychic messages that can be complex and foreign. Being able to understand this language, known as Dreamtongue, is critical to fully grasp exactly what is an Empath.

While all of us have a physical body, it does not essentially mean that we experience everything in life the same way. If you think about it this way, then you might focus on how you are born into different environments and how these environments act as the defining factor.

However, by not looking through the factors that may explain as to why people see life in different perspectives, there are also differences in terms of what's going on within someone. Just because a person has the same physical body, it does not automatically mean that they carry the same level of empathy as you.

You will meet people who have what is known as a balanced sense of empathy, and then, there are also the ones that are considered as out of balance. A person could be in a position where they have no empathy at all or too much empathy.

Non-existent empathy

When someone doesn't have empathy, they're not going to be a danger to themselves. Instead, they're likely to be a great danger to people around them. And they might even end up being classed as a psychopath. This kind of people can be found in prison and also in the corporate world wearing ties.

A person's lack of empathy could then be the reason as to why they ended up being in jail, and at the same time, it might also be the reason how they were able to find their way up to their job position. Having no empathy isn't going to help someone in terms of building relationships, but it can definitely help them in certain parts of their life.

Too much empathy

In contrary to someone who lacks empathy, someone who has too much empathy is unlikely to be a danger to others. Instead, they could be a great danger to themselves. And while they're not likely to be labeled cold, people would think they are oversensitive or even a push-over.

It's normal for them to do their best to avoid environments where there's too much going on and spend a lot of time on their own. If you see them in a room by themselves sitting silently, don't feel bad for them because they are there by choice.

On the other hand, they have a trait that helps them have deeper connections with others and bring warmth to their lives, but then again, it could also be a cause for an empath to avoid others. Because, as mentioned earlier, it could be too overwhelming for them to be around people a lot as such situations that involve many people could heighten their senses.

Out of Control

Having empathy is a trait that a person carries, but having this trait alone doesn't define that person. But then again, when a person has a high level of empathy, it could be something that can define how their lives are going to be.

For some, having a high level of empathy is a curse, and they don't really like it about themselves. Unfortunately, this is a tendency very hard to control, if not impossible, to control. What one can do about it is to embrace it and enjoy its benefits.

Sense of Self

When an empath is around others, it would not be easy for them to keep their sense of self. And the reason for this is that they tend to embody what's happening around them and what's going on inside them tend to be a mystery.

Actually, you may find it hard to differentiate between what they really feel and what they feel because of other people. Another thing about them is that they are easily adaptable. Their characteristics may change depending on who they are with.

4.1 Turning Empathy into Your Strength

We have a problem in the modern world that requires a solution.

It affects a big part of the world population, but it's so ingrained in our culture that it is easy for us to overlook how threatening it can be.

What is the problem? It is the denial of sensitivity.

We usually connect sensitivity with weakness, but by learning how to manage our energy and emotions, it's not that difficult to become more driven and control this unique trait.

Most people despise their sensitivity, not knowing that it is an extremely powerful root of productive energy when one learns how to accept it and use it positively.

For a big part of my life, I'd feel emotions very strongly – whether it was while watching emotional movies or seeing someone upset. I'd say being empathetic is just natural for me.

Unfortunately, there was a time I had to blend in with current's society – I cut these feelings off at the source, trying to intellectualize everything and separate my head from my body.

However, eventually, I realized that the more I avoided these feelings, particularly negative ones, the more and longer they would persist. I found that it was almost impossible to get rid of things. It was not uncommon for unsettled issues that I had not thought about in years to come up in a dream.

Now with the help of mindfulness practices and meditation, I have learned how to manage my emotions and use my sensitivity to be steered by my gut, feel more happiness, and use all that emotional energy in creative and positive ways.

Why do we see sensitivity as a bad thing?

Based on researcher Elaine Aron, around 15% to 20% of the population are very sensitive. This is because of the nature of their nervous systems. The people within this bracket usually have a predisposition toward emotional reactivity, overstimulation, as well as empathy.

It really doesn't bother me as to whether I fall this group or not. But I find it quite interesting how our society usually finds it culturally unsuitable to experience or show sensitivity.

How do you turn sensitivity into your strength?

There are many ways of doing this, and it is partially dependent on you as a person how you do it. However, there's one more important point to remember, and that is to accept who you are and the emotions you feel, not to curb or avoid them or to feel bad for simply experiencing them.

Avoidance and repression usually lead to what we knew as meta-emotions, emotions regarding emotions, like being mad because you're feeling sad, or feeling guilty for feeling too happy or excited.

What you want to do is to try to avoid these negative feelings at all costs, as they can truly be dangerous and confusing. Just accept the emotions as they are – they are absolutely normal.

Lately, I had an experience wherein I found myself doing this. I caught myself in a social situation feeling irritated with someone else's behavior. I then became disapproving of my own frustration – it did not fit with my self-perception as a laidback and collected person – and this turned into being angry at myself.

After a few minutes of dealing with pointless undesirable meta-emotions, I managed to catch myself and gather that being frustrated is okay. I'm just human, and this emotion is normal for any human being.

Sitting with your emotions

Most of us have different types of conscious or unconscious avoidance behaviors which stop us from experiencing both negative and positive emotions. Our sensitivity could make it seem like the experiences are extremely overwhelming, and we tend to cut them off.

This could be something as simple as getting distracted by the internet to stop thinking about your problems to avoiding your responsibilities at work or drinking or taking drugs in order to numb yourself from what's going on in your life.

For me, personally, one of the most effective ways is reading books, specifically the ones about philosophy, psychology, or spirituality. This activity helps me a lot. I was intellectualizing or ignoring any provoking emotions I was experiencing. This trick gave me a way to deal with those emotions without actually dealing with them.

I would also find myself saying yes to new projects or other opportunities because, at the time, they felt like a quick solution to any feelings that are too uncomfortable for me.

In order to counteract this tendency, which all of us might be experiencing at some point, we have to recognize the emotion when it's there, accept it and try to live with it, nonjudgmentally, and bodily sit with it for a moment and then let it go.

Use Your Passion and Creativity

A trait that usually goes with being sensitive is being creative and passionate.

Sensitive people tend to be artists, and vice versa, as they're more conscious of their emotions and it's easier for them to express their emotions through their work. Unfortunately, traditionally, education tends to give more important technical and business-related knowledge from an early age, and this encourages younger generations to give up their creative endeavors.

If you're passionate about something, it's important not to recede from following it, regardless of what anyone else says. You must make the most of any strong feelings you have, and use them as a compass that tells you what you need and what you want.

Sit back and reflect

People that are highly sensitive tend to be extremely reflective because as you already know, it's easy for them to get overwhelmed under extreme situations.

This is something we can use to our advantage. It's highly beneficial to engage in reflective practices like painting and writing and letting ourselves have some time to allow for our batteries to get recharged.

By simply taking some time out of the day to stop and reflect, whether that be in nature or just at home, it's easier for us to be more aware of the situation and the light nuances that are affecting us in our daily lives.

It's never healthy to suppress our sensitivity. In fact, it can even be destructive. If we only learn to deal with it, we can definitely use these practices to our advantage and let it be one of our major strengths.

Control empathy

3 Quick Ways to Get Control of Overactive Empathy

Do you know that moment when you get a sight of someone else's emotional experience or agony? You could really feel it a little bit, and sometimes, it may put you to tears or encourage you to give a helping hand. That is empathy.

On the other hand, too much empathy is when you have that experience opening up to the experience and emotions of someone else, but then rather than coming back to yourself after that, your concerns and thoughts remain at the same place – you get absorbed in other people's stuff too much. When it comes to social situations, you are able to sense what other people around you are thinking and feeling. Even by simply walking past people in the street, you are capable of feeling and sensing what's going on around them. Meanwhile, for physical empaths, they can even feel physical pains that are not theirs.

The Problem with Overactive Empathy

As your energy absorbs energy and adapts to what other people are doing and feeling, your life gets charged with pain and emotions that are not even yours, and it becomes harder for you to keep a state of focus or centeredness. On the other hand, your own needs can go entirely unaddressed.

Intense empathy can result in self-sacrifice, people-pleasing, and self-neglect. It can also result in co-dependence as when you can feel the emotions of others to such a level, they become yours, and you may end up needing help more than the others.

This is something that many psychic and spiritual individuals struggle with.

If you experience overactive empathy, it's important for you to learn how to turn it on and off and to get yourself to be the center of your concern. And fortunately, it's not as hard as it sounds. And when you finally learn how to do it, it's surely going to make your life a thousand times better. Believe me; I'm speaking from my experience.

Now, using these three tips I'm going to give you, it's going to be easier for you to manage your unique trait and even use it to your advantage.

1. Pay Enough Attention to How You Feel

In order to overcome empathy, you have to focus back to YOU. For you to get centered, you have to check in with yourself emotionally every once in a while and observe the way you feel things. Before going to bed, you can make a log of how you feel and what's the reason behind those feelings. When someone asks a favor, make sure to check in with how you feel about it first before saying yes. Don't base your answer on what they're going to feel if they don't hear what they want to hear. Always take your precious time to become the main focus of your life and for your feelings to prevail. Sometimes, your own feelings regarding things take time to get through when you are too focused on the needs of others.

As mentioned earlier, meditation could also be a good tool that will help you focus on yourself. But this will only be effective when you do it on a regular basis and imagine recollecting the energy back that you gave to others. Every time I feel like my energy is out of order and ungrounded, I usually imagine my energy coming back to me. I imagine my energy in the form of beaming lights coming into my body. Having this kind of visualization simply sets the intention of bringing your energy back to you and can have a placebo effect.

2. Make it a habit to ask

Every time you feel overwhelmed with emotion or feel like you lost yourself in connections with others, you can always take three deep, long breaths, and then chime a little prayer asking the higher power to help you remove all the energies that do not belong to you and all the energies that belong to you to come back to their right place.

Do a little prayer that truly comes from the heart? It does not have to be too long and complicated. It could consist of three sentences. This is a simple yet powerful way to successfully retrieve your lost energy.

3. Give yourself permission to enjoy yourself

Most empaths can't have experiences when they interact with others. They tend to have the feeling that they're here to help others that are experiencing sufferings. They usually feel submissive and feel responsible for the feelings of others.

In order to fix this, it's important to focus on having fun during an interaction with others. During social situations, if you are not having fun, leave or talk to someone else who you think you will enjoy with. It's better to pull back than spending your time around people who do nothing except draining your energy. Prioritize your own enjoyment during social situations and don't pay too much attention to other people than you normally would. While this might sound a little bit selfish, this will help you improve your life significantly.

Chapter 5

COMMON DANGERS IN THE LIFE OF AN EMPATH

As natural born healers, empaths are heavily affected by the energy of the people around them. They have an inborn ability to naturally feel and recognize the emotions of others, providing them with a keen sense of knowing when people carry good or bad intentions. A lot of people might see them as weak people as they're very vulnerable to human emotions. While empaths usually cope with the pressure of their own emotions together with other peoples, weak is not a word to describe them.

Empaths are sensitive people, but not in a bad way. They have a deep sensitivity to radio broadcasts, television, and even the internet. Emotional dramas and violence portraying shocking and harsh scenes of emotional and physical pain can usually be agonizing for an empath. They have a deep ability to have patience with people that often gets them to get taken advantage of. Empaths usually see the good in others, and it could get the best of them sometimes. However, being an empath comes with dangers.

Empaths are most attractive to negative energies, no matter how much they want to attract positive energies more. It seems like escaping the evils of the world is almost impossible, which gives them an even deeper knowledge of how the world really works. This understanding could usually scare or upset empaths. They take in this negative energy, and it takes a toll on them, which causes them to always look exhausted or fatigued.

Empaths tend to neglect their mind and body just for the sake of others. They have a dark understanding with them that's very heavy. When they start neglecting themselves, it forms up over time and makes them lose their sense of self. Once an empath falls in love, they cannot entirely let themselves be helpless. They could never let go of everything in their heart to someone else. If they did, it could potentially make the relationship overwhelming and intense for both parties.

Being an empath should be considered as a gift and not a curse. Don't let the negative energies of others control your perspective. Don't let yourself mask in the emotional energy of others – it doesn't end well.

If we grow up knowing and appreciating our real natures, we do not get so captivated in other people's troubles. It's when we don't comprehend what's going on, and we fight and resist all the emotional troubles that we start our ultimate struggle with being an empath, and it could be our curse to carry.

So, the question is, can we change that?

When I was young, I got serious anxiety when my birthday approaches; I would cry secretly in my room because I am getting older, and to me, it means getting closer to dying. Do you know any kid who is also afraid of dying? Or even someone who just thinks about it?

I felt like as I grow old, the more I struggle about my emotions. If I get 1 dollar for every time someone tells me I'm too sensitive or to stop crying over "petty" things, I'd be so rich by now.

So, I did my best to just bottle it up.

Many years passed, and I always felt heavy, not understanding why my joy or happiness was so brief. Feelings of grief would come to stay. I felt increasingly more blah, without actual attachment to anything and not finding fulfillment.

I loved watching movies growing up, well, until now, and a lot of movies I watch would make me cry easily when the characters are experiencing grief. Some of my friends would think I'm silly crying of something they thought was shallow.

At first, I wanted to do something to change myself because I wanted to "fit in." But as I grew older, I started to see the good things about this trait, so instead of changing myself for them, I just tried to find ways to protect myself from the negativities people threw at me.

These are the things I follow daily, and if I don't follow them for several days, I notice a change and make sure I find time for them.

Meditation. One of the best things you can do for yourself is to start your morning with meditation as it sets the tone for the whole day. It can help you be more content, focused, and positive. Set aside at least 10 minutes a day first thing in the morning and be ready to face your day with clarity.

Get Your Neurons on Fire. If you depend waking up on your alarm clock, then the routine of your mind will tend to be slow. Start your morning with brain stimulation and get your neurons going. Try to use something else to wake you up that will make your brain associate all forms of positivity with them. Rather than using an alarm, may be pre-set the coffee maker to start brewing your coffee for you as you wake up.

Get Your Mind in the State of Gratitude. When you wake up in the morning, start listing all the things you are feeling thankful for that day. Doing this will make your brain just focus on the positive things. You'll rewire your attitude to a positive state and so ruining your day will almost be impossible. Doing this will also help you reduce your stress and improve your quality of life and overall health.

Focus on What You Want to Achieve. Start your day with the intention of doing your best and attaining greatness. Following a daily routine can be helpful, but having it on its own is not enough. You should hold yourself responsible for your success. Have a small journal with you not only to write the things you are grateful for but also the things you want to achieve on that day. Making this a habit will train your mind to concentrate on that which aligns most with the things you are passionate about.

Chapter 6

Overcoming Your Fears

There are many reasons you might feel lost as a highly empathetic person. But fortunately, there are also some easy ways to overcome these feelings.

1. Distinguishing your own pain and of others is hard

Sometimes, as empaths, we experience a wave of overpowering emotion coming from other people. We are waiting in line for our coffee, and the next thing we know is that we are suddenly anguished from a person next to us. This is something that is truly painful.

If it's so easy for empaths to be affected by emotions of people they don't know, then imagine how it is going to be for them if people who are closer to them are involved. These situations can make empaths to be fearful and nervous, as they never know when they will experience these agonizing feelings. They can consciously or unconsciously try to numb their senses to stop them from feeling so intensely.

They can also be pretty reclusive in their efforts to evade the emotions of other people. This is a shame as they also miss out on sharing fun and excitement with others.

Many times, they feel sad and miserable without knowing what the real reason is. If they can't distinguish their own feelings from that of others, they will absorb stress and pain around them all the time and suffer from being exhausted and overwhelmed. This can lead to unexplainable mood swings and changing energy levels. This also triggers physical symptoms like fatigue and headaches.

It's not really surprising why empaths usually feel lost and are trying to numb themselves to these powerful emotions. Unfortunately, trying to numb ourselves to pain can also numb joy and make us feel more miserable.

What to do

So, in order to overcome this, the first thing you need to do is to distinguish our own pain from the pain of other people around us. As mentioned earlier, meditating would be the best way to do it.

When you can successfully know what pain belongs to you and what pain belongs to others, dealing with emotions would be the next thing you need to do. Being able to know which emotions don't belong to you doesn't mean you need to be cold and uncaring. You can still be yourself and be your caring self like you've always been, but know your boundaries.

In order to get started on clearing the energies of other people from yourself, taking a sea salt bath would help significantly. This is very beneficial in clearing away energies that aren't yours and grounds you back into your own body. The moment you feel that there are harmful energies around you, you can use incense or sage smudging to dispel them. Another thing that can help you is spending time with nature.

If you happen to be in a situation where you know you'll be spending time with those who are distressed and experiencing pain, you may want to practice a protection meditation ahead of time. You can do this by sitting in a comfortable, upright position and take a few deep breaths. Then visualize yourself being surrounded by bright light. Stay in this light breathing deeply for a few more minutes. You are able to count your breaths if it's hard for you to stay focused as your mind wanders around a lot.

2. You try to hinder or lessen your sensitivity to blend in

I'm sure you're a victim of the remark, "You're too sensitive!" Maybe, you've been diagnosed with anxiety or some sort of mood disorder. People might have even said that you are 'too much' or even silly.

Of course, when someone makes us feel unaccepted because of the emotions we express, we tend to feel lost and try to conceal our sensitive natures and stuff down the feelings that others find so hard to handle. We try to conform and be seen as "normal" by everyone around us.

What to do

If ever you feel lost because you've avoided your real emotions, you have to work on loving and respecting yourself. A lot of people are empaths, but not all of them see their trait as a gift. Empaths are amazing when it comes to reconciling other people, reducing friction, and fixing disagreements.

Of course, they're also extremely caring and usually work to help others, animals, and anything in the world that has a life. Sometimes, accepting an aspect of our empathetic nature can be a means of healing ourselves. Empaths love the idea of being a volunteer at a charity, rescuing abandoned animals, or offering to a cause that they believe in.

The main key to overpowering the feelings of being not enough or being different, that an empath living in modern society can feel, is acceptance. Seek sources that you can get support from, whether by venting to others, reading a book about the subject, or connecting to people on the internet.

You may also want to try writing down all the good things about yourself and all the accomplishments you've made. Usually, you focus on things that you did wrong and fail to notice and give enough credit to your strengths and achievements. Another great way to achieve self-acceptance is to look at yourself in the mirror, look yourself right in the eye, and talk to yourself. Tell yourself you love the person who is looking at you.

3. You had a bad or erratic childhood

A lot of empaths developed their skills as an essential survival skill when they were still a child. If you grew up around adults who were unpredictable, violent, or emotionally unstable, you'd have developed the skills of reading every change in their mood and emotions. This helped you avoid the situation if it gets bad.

What to do?

If you feel lost due to your childhood, you have to work on your feelings of insecurity and vulnerability. You're not at the mercy of the emotions of others. If anyone acts in a way that offends you, there's nothing wrong with walking away. But of course, all relationships have their own ups and downs. Due to each person's experiences, any form of argument or confrontation can make you feel scared, weak, alone, and lost.

Any grounding practices are able to help you feel secure and safe. Spend more time doing what you want, things that you truly enjoy and bring you genuine happiness.

Here are also other grounding techniques you may want to follow:

Stand up straight with your feet on the ground all the time. Visualize a bright white light coming from the top of your head, going down to your spine, then further down to your legs. Then start imagining this light oozing out beneath your feet. This light is the foundation you have to remain grounded. Tell yourself repeatedly, 'I'm safe and secure' over and over again as you take a deep breath.

If you're an empath or a very sensitive person, then it is important to know that there are effective and crucial ways for you to guide yourself and protect your energy.

Your capability to feel and understand the emotions of other people, as well as your surroundings, might also mean that you're also vulnerable to the energetic imprint of people around you.

This is how to protect yourself effectively, and without coming from a place of worry, fear, or despise.

Being an empath means you literally feel what other people are experiencing emotionally. You are able to feel it within your body and how you show your mood, feelings, and your thoughts. You could also feel it determinedly and on a delicate level without even realizing it.

Whatever is considered as negativity in general, particularly when it comes to our energetic surroundings, really simply goes down to the toxicity of the environment.

Some of this toxicity can literally come from anything – from the foods we consume, people we work with, news we read, people we live with, emotions we feel, thoughts we think, things we do, and the burden for resources that we associate as daily life.

While there are many toxins you can acquire, sometimes, they also come directly from other people. This is something that is called emotional energy pollution.

Whatever we feel around us has a great range of vibrations within it, and if we choose to carry this emotional energy pollution, it could literally bring us down. The energy we have is very dense and even less harmonic.

There is a bigger chance for empaths to not just feel the emotional energy of others, but also to take it on as a way to process it. This is something empaths can do both knowingly or unknowingly.

According to several studies, empaths are a lot likely to have social anxiety, depression, introversion, and loneliness. It is necessary for empaths to know the best ways to manage all the negative energy coming in their everyday life.

Whether you're an empath or not, negativity is a very powerful force, and once it begins compounding in your life, all things in your life get bad and ugly. It's always a good idea to apply consistently in your life in order to avoid being stuck in a prison that you create.

Here are the better choices you may want to follow:

1) Create strong boundaries

Since empaths are known to be more sensitive to their surroundings and other people's emotional energies, it can usually mean they're more absorbent towards their environment, just like how a sponge is.

And if not carefully managed, it can potentially affect your decisions, willpower, behavior, and habits. This also means that the energetic, personal, mental, and emotional boundaries can be compromised.

This is not good. Always keep in mind that you're an independent human being with free will. It's your life, so it also means that it's your responsibility and you're free to make choices and decisions. In a way, you have to stand guard at the gates of the different levels of your being, not afraid and aware of what is truly yours and not.

So, what's going to happen if you don't maintain healthy boundaries? Well, as an empath, the emotions of others, their problems, and all the noise pollution from the media and local news are likely to steal your presence. Negativity will start to force in and consume things, and it's always up to you if you are preventing it or you're just going to live with it.

Pro Tip: Figure out when you should say "Yes" and "No". Practice it and maintain it; it is surely one of the best tools you will ever learn to develop your internal boundaries.

2) Acknowledge Your Needs

There used to be a time when I'd find myself sitting around contemplating everything that I wanted, but completely naive about what I really needed.

The moment I came to this shocking realization, I was woken up to the fact I was tremendously using my energy in the wrong direction. So first of all, I had to acknowledge that I was obstructing so much in my life from flowing just because I was distancing myself from my needs.

One of the best things you can learn as an empath is that once you figure out what your needs are, you will also start to learn how to openly communicate them in a well-adjusted way with others who you need in fulfilling your needs.

What Maslow's Hierarchy of Needs teaches us is that until we meet our basic needs, we're totally limited in objectifying the higher levels of existence.

This means that if your basic needs of food, rest, shelter, clothing, and survival aren't met, you're strictly limited in growing your consciousness or spiritual achievement, along with material affluence in the physical world.

So, as an empath or a person with a higher level of sensitivity, you have to work out what your needs are and communicate them into your life if you want to thrive and grow.

If you choose not to communicate your needs, there is a great chance for negativity to build up in your life and make things excessively challenging. You begin to live a life made of the needs of others instead of your own.

3) Don't be afraid to use your time and space when necessary

They say that no man is an island, and while this is true to some extent, this is something that doesn't apply to an empath. Empath doesn't feel lonely for being alone. In fact, many of them feel lonely when surrounded by people who they don't enjoy due to personality differences. So, for many empaths, keeping a distance from people makes them feel alive.

But don't get me wrong! This is not to shy away from the importance of having amazing, healthy environments and social communities. Interactions are still one of the main needs of empaths as human beings. But at the same time, taking healthy space and distance from other people is important to settle back into themselves.

4) Take note of what's draining you

As mentioned earlier, empaths tend to be very intuitive. Intuitive energy is usually associated with the capability to read other people's intentions and emotions. This is something that has been attested to have healing and spiritual benefits, but it also has the possible setback that some intuitive gifts have.

It's best to live your life by your intuition. Create a call and response relationship based on your intuition. Let it guide you in making your choices, environments, and new surroundings.

You are able to save yourself from going through so much negativity when you just don't do the things that are draining you.

As empaths, we tend to choose to have bleeding hearts just to relieve the pain of others because it feels as if it makes us feel better.

And honestly, this is a foolish approach and not the best way to encourage someone to grow. This is something that roots from ego and insecurity, and the negativity that can be present behind it.

5) Develop energetic cleansing and protection rituals

It's important for empaths to cleanse themselves from the negative energy they pick up on a day to day basis.

This could also be a part of the time they allow themselves to recoup and rejuvenate and come home to themselves. This can range from long periods of time to daily maintenance.

It's important to cleanse both emotional energy and negative energy pollution we collect, just as we need to take a shower after a long, tiring day. Then we need to process the emotions beneath this energy.

Although it might be from the outside world, we still need to own it. We need to be aware of what's the lesson for us to learn, as this exists in our lives with reason and purpose.

Here are some cleansing methods you can follow to successfully protect yourself:

- ❖ Expose yourself to the sun and nature
- ❖ Ground your feet on the earth
- ❖ Take a bath with scented candles
- ❖ Use essential oil regularly
- ❖ Pray and meditate
- ❖ Have a healthy, daily routine
- ❖ Quit internet temporarily

❖ Practice gratitude

Each of us is on a continuous journey to improving ourselves and not trying to throw back the negativity into the world.

Basically, as an empath, embracing incredible difficulty and rising through it and transforming it might be a part of who you are as a person.

By finding a way to plug into the world's emotional energy, you become a barometer for initiating the changes you want in the world. You play a great, amazing role. And just like all any other good gifts in the world, all of them need an application of effort, attention, and love to nurture.

Chapter 7

Protecting Yourself as an Empath – Setting Boundaries

So, how do you set good boundaries with people without making yourself isolated? This is definitely a vital question as you're learning how to deal with a world filled with people who have become accustomed to sucking the energy of others rather than making their own. If you would like to become truly autonomous, then you have to know when to give and when to guard your energy.

In terms of boundaries, we're all aware of how important that is. Depending on your personality, keeping healthy boundaries might be uncomfortable, confusing, and even absolutely embarrassing.

Some people are very clear when it comes to what they want. They have a strong list of rules that make for a strong boundary between them and negativities they want to keep themselves away from. These people are usually the ones who can easily say, "No, thanks. Maybe next time." or "I'm sorry, but I'm currently busy, and this is my priority for now."

On the other hand, some people lack boundaries; they hardly notice how silly they look trying very hard at all times and apologizing for everything they do. They always walk on eggshells and doing everything just to please other people. "Oh, okay, just let me finish this quickly, and I'll do it," "Of course, I can do it for you," or "Sure, yes, I will definitely make time for it."

Realistically, it is possible to be in excesses on either end. Just like most things in life, the middle path is the better way. We cannot be very firm on our boundaries that we fail to spread ourselves in reciprocation and make the intimate relationships we as human beings need. Similarly, not having boundaries is putting yourself into disaster, stress, or a total meltdown.

For people who are trying to learn how to have healthy boundaries without isolating themselves from others, it is important to keep in mind that every day, we are the ones who set our relationships on how they are.

Whether you believe it or not, your friends are probably not needy with their other friends. They just knew that you'd always say yes and they are taking advantage of it. Now, it's in your hands whether you want to change that or not.

Value Yourself

Your time is not worth less than others.

To start the journey toward building healthy boundaries, the first thing you need to do is welcome the mindset that you are important, no less than other people around you. This means that your time, emotions, and efforts should be given importance too.

Regardless of what you want to do with your free time, whether it is to volunteer, go to the salon, watch movies, take a nap, or go somewhere you've always wanted to go, it's entirely up to you. No one is in a position to tell you how you should manage your time aside from you. When you are dealing with people who don't give importance to your time, then you have to do something about it. It doesn't matter if your friends need someone to make coffee for them while they are busy doing a project if you are also hasting to finish a project. If you are looking forward to the weekend because you want to start a new project, which might be painting or home organization when suddenly a friend calls asking you to come over, don't be afraid to say no if you don't feel like going.

If you really want to help your friends with something, then it's okay. But if you are too willing to do something for others to the point that it is affecting your own happiness and desires, then you really need to reconsider your decisions.

Any relationship that doesn't have a mutual exchange of energy in the form of love, attention, time, resources and the like must be questioned. While you should not be keeping an emotional equilibrium of what someone has or has not done for you, if you're starting to notice that the relationship is a one-way street, and that you find that people are always expecting you to be there for them whenever they need you, when they hardly ever extend the same courtesy, then it might be a sign that they are not the only ones who are not respecting your boundaries, but also YOU.

Within a healthy family, these boundaries are set up at a very young age. When we are young, we start to learn that our feelings, thoughts, and emotions are very important. Similarly, we learn the importance of respecting the opinions, ideas, and emotions of others.

If you grew up in a family that is considered dysfunctional, alcoholic, or co-dependent, then you might grow up feeling not good enough, and no matter what you do, it's not going to be enough. You learned that your role is to please everyone.

You did this to have fulfilled the missing part of you when you were a child— to be noticed, appreciated, and loved. Within an average family, boundaries are usually accepted and honored even, and individuals then make interactions with the rest of the world with that principle in place. Growing up in a dysfunctional family, there's a big chance for you to attract people who constantly dominate your need for energetic independence as this might seem what's normal to you.

Healthy Boundaries in Every Relationship

Whether it is social boundaries or boundaries within intimate relationships, it is worth noting that it's essential to make sure that you're doing things for the right reasons. Now that we've established what healthy boundaries are and their importance let's now talk about why keeping them can be difficult for some, especially for highly empathetic persons.

First of all, if building boundaries is something that is new to you, then you're probably used to keeping yourself away from conflict, hating awkward silence, or seeing someone struggling. Perhaps, you're someone with just have an extreme fear of missing out. Well, these traits perfectly describe some people that are highly empathetic.

When you're just starting to develop healthy boundaries, being a little messy at first is normal. It's pretty normal to give yourself a pep talk in your head before saying yes or no to a request.

As a highly empathetic person, this can be an enormous challenge. You get deeply emotional whether the problems are your own or someone else's. This empathy is domineering for many people to evolve past war and constant conflict, but don't expect everyone else will feel what you feel and will show the same level of empathy; you'll just get hurt.

You will encounter people who will use your empathy in order to get what they want from you, without thinking about what you will feel. There's no sense of mutuality, and so a healthy relationship is impossible, at least until they learn how to respect others the way they want to be respected.

The moment you begin setting healthy boundaries, you might find yourself being busy explaining every reason as to why you are not choosing to do something, usually making people think that you are not being honest with them about why you suddenly said NO when they know as a Yes man, and you may even hear people saying something negative about you behind your back. But that's alright. You don't owe others an explanation unless you are getting paid, you committed to doing it, and/or you signed a contract to do it.

Keep in mind that starting to refuse things might be harder for you than those people who you refused to say yes to. So, be kind to yourself and remind yourself that you are doing it for yourself this time. This will surely be a journey, and you need to be patient with yourself. Soon enough, you'll find a middle ground where you do not always have to say no, and you're not going to be in a situation where you need to explain yourself for choosing what you want.

Healthy Emotional Habits

Building boundaries comes with having healthy habits. If you already made up your mind and decided to build boundaries, then you should be ready to destroy your destructive habits and replace them with healthier ones. Some of the bad habits you need to let go include saying sorry too much, easily giving in when someone said "please," offering help even when not being asked, and sacrificing your needs for others.

You have to remember that most successful habit changes require the coordination of different strategies to create a single new behavior, and new habits, averagely, take about 2 months to form, so the more strategies you used, the better it is going to be. Creating new habits requires a plan because your brain prefers to save energy and carry on doing what it has always done before.

So, while your established desire to make healthy boundaries might have you thinking, "I am worth it, and people will see that" you might still abate to maintain them until the new habit of honoring yourself gets more cohesive.

An excellent strategy for creating healthy boundaries will address the realities of why you're failing to have any limits in the first place. Practice rewiring your negative beliefs about yourself. For example, create a list of legitimate reasons why you always choose to say yes or why is it hard for you to say no. After that, start writing them in reverse in order to turn them into positive statements as to how you really want to act and feel. Turn these into positive statements, and commit to reading them as a part of your everyday routine to remind yourself what you should do.

A great reason to have boundaries, oddly enough, involves having good emotional habits.

If building boundaries is part of your struggle, then this will be a long road ahead. To make things more organized, you can create a vision board or give yourself some time to sit and contemplate on your goals, dreams, and desires, and perhaps make a to-do list where you write your upcoming plans. Who knows, you might even discover new hobbies that you would actually enjoy.

Try to make space to better yourself rather than persistently rushing to fix everyone else. Make a list of things you have not done alone before. Maybe go to the cinema alone, eat at your favorite restaurant alone, travel alone, or simply create things that you haven't tried without involving others. Be selfish, but in a good way. By doing things independently, you will see how easy it is to be alone sometimes, and therefore, you will realize that people might not even need your presence. With this in mind, it's going to be easier for you to refuse their request when you don't want to do it.

Prepare Yourself for Common Pitfalls

No one can assure what's going to happen next. Once again, it's going to be hard at first – after all, you'll always be the same, kind-hearted person who's willing to give out as much as he can. So, you in order to be successful at your journey to building boundaries, you need to make a plan when pitfalls are met.

Situation: So, you decided to make a change this morning, but then your co-worker asked you to have lunch with her because she doesn't want to eat out alone. You still went with her even though you would rather finish something first – you could have told her to wait a few more minutes, but you didn't want her to wait.

What you could have done: You told her that you're still finishing something. If she could wait for about 15 more minutes, you might be able to go. Otherwise, she could try with someone else.

Now, figure out what you did wrong. Find the reason. You didn't want her to wait; that's why you said yes. Write it down on a piece of paper. Read it. Then read it slowly. Read it more until you realize how silly that reason is. She's a grown woman who could wait. If you could wait to eat lunch as you need to finish work, then she could.

If you start doing this practice of writing down what went wrong on your journey to building boundaries, you may find how you've been neglecting self-care. You will see how you've gotten caught in the web of being a pushover.

Again, list down situations you believe that hindered your plans of creating boundaries, and next to those situations, write things that you wish could have had happened.

There are endless ways to say no without offending someone. By planning ahead and trying things out, it's going to be easy for you to only say yes to things that you genuinely want.

Summing it up

It's possible to build healthy boundaries, even if you're an intuitive, super-caring, empathetic person. You can still be the same, helpful person, but without compromising your own needs and desires. Once you successfully build the healthy boundaries that will help you to be a better person for yourself, you will also start to have a healthier relationship with others and slowly, you will regain your lost energy. It is totally worth it to develop healthy boundaries, even with your friends and families.

Rather than always playing emotional tug-of-war with other people, it's a smart idea to build boundaries that will help you gain respect from yourself and from others.

7.1 The Relationship between an Empath and Narcissist

Did you know that empaths and narcissists are attracted to each other? So, why is this? The combination of these two personality traits could result in a perilous and toxic relationship, and let me tell you why.

A narcissist is someone who's self-absorbed and lacks the capability to empathize with people around them.

Especially in the society we live in today, and with the rise of social media and materialism, everyone could be a bit narcissistic at some point. It's a personality trait that exists everywhere. However, if we are talking about full-blown clinical level, Narcissistic Personality Disorder is a mental disorder that harshly damages healthy functioning. A person who has this disorder tends to use other people as a way to fulfill their own needs and desires and disregard their feelings.

That is the total opposite of an empath. In contrast to the traits of a narcissist, an empath finds it so easy to relate to the feelings of others, actually so much, that they can easily feel what others can.

They usually care for others without thinking about themselves. An empath can actually feel other people's emotions, physical symptoms, and energy without the use of common defenses that most people have.

Now, you're probably confused and asking: So, why would two such different individuals even find each other attractive?

Well, this is a case of opposites attract.

Both personalities have what the other person wants, and when coming together, instead of helping each other, it's a toxic relationship.

An empath needs a person that they can take care of. Meanwhile, a narcissist can sense this and take advantage of it by manipulating the empath for his own interests. Narcissists tend to be extremely charismatic and can even fake love and care when they know that it will help them get what they want.

Essentially, a narcissist is a wounded person. There are times when the disorder roots from early childhood experiences if they didn't experience love and attention growing up. They will then start to crave the validation and attention from others but will be incapable of offering genuine love back.

As the natural caretakers, empaths can easily sense this underlying wound and would want to do everything within their powers to please the narcissist. What they might not notice is how the narcissist is a taker and feed on the empath like an energy vampire.

The more attention the empath gives to the narcissist, the more exhausted he becomes.

Of all people, the empath can usually sense that their partner is a narcissist. Similarly, they can also usually sense if their partner is not capable of loving them back. However, the problem is that, just like an abusive relationship, it could be quite challenging to escape the cycle of attraction and destruction. Whenever the empath gets hurt, they'll find themselves isolated as the narcissist is not capable of giving them the comfort they need. Furthermore, they will be very good at shifting blame for misdoings away from themselves, further victimizing their partner.

No matter how bad it gets, the empath will hold on because they think that they can heal the narcissist. They do not want to leave the narcissist alone, people with no social skills like empaths, because what will come of them?

It's crucial for the empath to realize that the narcissist is wounded to the point of no return. They simply do not have the innate ability to empathize. The empath must get out of the relationship before further abuse wears their self-esteem and energy down further. **It will not get better; it will only get worse.**

And the narcissist, being incapable of empathy, will not be the one with the sense to put an end to the abusive relationship.

7.1.1 Different Types of Narcissists Every Empath Should Look Out For

There are a lot of articles that are talking about "protecting" yourself from narcissists. However, what I see wrong with them is how they promote the disempowering idea that "other people are out to get you." Well, they are not.

Most people act within the limits of their conscious capacity, and sometimes that involves hurting other people. The more you see yourself as a "victim" of narcissists, the less capable you will be of truly owning your personal power as an empath.

A significant part of owning this personal power is to learn how to identify different types of narcissists there are. The more aware you are of these different types, the more deliberately you will be able to act and take action in their presence.

Main Types of Narcissists

Fascinatingly, there are two main types of narcissists:

Vulnerable Narcissists

Generally, these people are very sensitive and tend to be shy and quiet by nature. Yet, in order to mask their chronic feelings of self-loathing and worthlessness, vulnerable narcissists overreact by putting on a lavish mask, looking to merge their identities with other idealized individuals. Vulnerable Narcissists have an unshakeable need to feel special about themselves and have little honest regard for the feelings of others. Vulnerable Narcissists are mainly driven by fear of abandonment and rejection. Thus, they do not have the capacity to genuinely give love and care for others. Furthermore, vulnerable narcissists use emotional manipulation to secure attention and sympathy from others. Their lives are powered by inferiority complexes that usually root from childhood abuse.

Invulnerable Narcissists

These individuals reflect the traditional personality of the narcissist: that of a highly-confident, unempathetic, and cold person. Invulnerable narcissists, unlike vulnerable narcissists, are thick-skinned and boldly seek power, recognition, glory, and desire. Invulnerable narcissists usually suffer from superiority complexes, seeing themselves to be far bigger than everyone else – and they have a compulsive need to make everyone know.

Both of these types share the same traits like using other people to fuel their narcissistic delusions, criticizing and blaming, lack of empathy, infidelity, and the desire for power.

Subtypes

Both vulnerable narcissistic and invulnerable narcissistic personality types can be separated into the following subtypes. Keep in mind that there are a lot of these subtypes that could overlap with each other:

The Amorous Narcissist

Amorous narcissists measure their splendor and self-worth by how many sexual defeats they have under their belt. This type of narcissist is well-known for using his charm to trap others with gifts and flattery, but then immediately getting rid of them when they become "boring" or they find a "replacement." Amorous narcissists are the ultimate relationship con artists, heart-breakers, and gold diggers. At first look, they may seem very attractive, charming, and amiable, but behind those, they're only out to satisfy and gratify their own desires and needs.

The Compensatory Narcissist

Compelled to make up for past traumas, compensatory narcissists love making false illusions of themselves and their accomplishments. For them to recuperate power and take over their lives, this type of narcissist frequently preys on emotionally vulnerable individuals who will become the audience to their made-up stage acts. In reality, this type of narcissist is very sensitive to criticism and will typically find negative self-directed hints from others. Manipulation and emotional abuse is their favorite way of controlling others.

The Elitist Narcissist

This type of person would have no problem with doing anything just to get to the top, win, and entirely dominate others. Elitist narcissists completely believe that they're better than usual because of their backgrounds and achievements and so they think that they deserve special treatment. Their sense of entitlement is felt and seen in every action they make. Embracing a severely overblown ego, elitist narcissists are experts when it comes to self-promoting, bragging, and one-uppers. They have an aggressive need to be labeled as "best" and prove themselves to be intelligently superior at all times no matter what happens.

The Malignant Narcissist

The behavior of malignant narcissists usually overlaps with that of psychopaths and people who have an antisocial personality disorder. Malignant narcissists generally have no respect or interest in moral and immoral behavior and don't feel sorrow for their actions. This subgroup is known as an arrogant and high sense of self-worth that pleasures in "outsmarting" other people. This type of narcissists can usually be found in gangs, prisons, and drug rehabilitation centers, even though a lot of them manage to get away from the law.

7.1.2 How to Deal with Narcissists

An empath may spend a lot of time being emotionally abused, manipulated, and disrespected by a narcissist, but this doesn't have to be the case. Here are some practical ways to deal with a narcissist.

1. Just DON'T

You probably heard the saying, "Prevention is better than cure." Well, this saying applies when dealing with a narcissist, and this is possibly the best advice you can follow.

Narcissists lack empathy, they usually don't work hard, and worse, they tend to make the life of people around them a nightmare. And narcissism is very difficult to change. So, as much as possible, just stay away from them.

2. Determine which type you're dealing with

Vulnerable narcissists do not feel necessarily good about themselves at heart. Contrary to grandiose narcissists, they are less "out there" with their emotions, and so you may not realize when they are weakening you or getting in your way. If you're trying to put people in your work team or family to use, the grandiose narcissist could be your best friend – as long as you could get that person involved with your overall goals of the group.

3. Acknowledge your annoyance

Narcissists can be aggressive and get under your skin. If you are trying to finish something, and a person is always intruding or trying to get the limelight on himself or herself, it will be helpful to recognize where the frustration is coming from. This can give you the strength you need to stop it all.

4. Kiss Up or Shut Up

Dealing with a narcissist that has power over you – for example, a boss – can be a bit trickier. So, what does Kiss up or Shut up even mean? It means just try to kiss them up or just say nothing to them until you get out of their presence. Trying to reduce the encounters with them is sometimes the next best choice.

5. Recognize that the person may need help

Because some narcissists genuinely have low self-esteem and profound feelings of inadequacy, it's important to recognize when they can benefit from professional intervention. Despite the belief that personality is immutable, psychotherapy research shows that people can change even long-standing behaviors. Bolstering the individual's self-esteem may not be something you can tackle on your own, but it is something you can work on with outside help.

Chapter 8

DEALING WITH EXHAUSTION AND FATIGUE

Empaths usually carry a heavy load with them throughout the day. Most of the time, highly sensitive people like empaths feel an intense level of unstable emotions in response to things happening around them. And to take in different emotions from different people at the same time, all day is just a great recipe for exhaustion.

The worse part of this exhaustion, however, is that escaping it is almost impossible. For an average person, lying down on the couch, listening to some good music, or sleeping for hours is enough to regain their energy. It's different for empaths.

Seclusion doesn't really help when you feel the emotions of the world or even the feelings of people in your inner circle, no matter where they are in the world.

Absorbing energy from walls, objects, the earth, or animals adds into this excess of emotions. Then you have those people who pick up emotions of spirits and energetic memories. Some empaths just feel like being secluded is just impossible.

The point is that everything around us is energy and empaths, being deeply affected by this energy, have little to no escape.

When all's said and done, as an empath crawls into bed, what they crave for is an emotional escape during their sleep, only to enter a feverish dream state: lucid dreams, bright colors, and vivid events of past, present, and future. Uncontrollable tornados of emotions tend to overtake their mental and physical state without conscious amnesty. Spiritual intruders, getting into their dream state, which even lures them to different places and out of body experiences.

Empaths usually find themselves waking up even more exhausted, stressed, and tensed than before they fell asleep.

How to find relief

Regardless of how miserable and hopeless this constant state of exhaustion might seem, you can always find a way to overcome this fatigue. As you start to look for relief by using the following tips, you have to be patient with yourself and know that it might take practice to overcome a lifetime of feeling exhausted.

Remember feeling refreshed

When you're engrossed in empath fatigue, dragging yourself through every moment, you may find it difficult to remember what it feels like to be bushy-tailed and bright-eyed. But everyone has had times in their lives when they've felt a higher level of energy. Try to remember those times, no matter how brief.

Maybe it was a feeling of excitement over traveling to another place that gave you a sudden burst of energy. Maybe, you can recall attending an event that really allowed you to enjoy and have fun. Try to remember as many times as you can when you felt relief from the stress.

Go deep into that memory and try to feel again how it felt to be refreshed and relaxed. Remember how your body felt, how your breath was eased. Recall the huge smile on your face; the real one, the one that takes no effort. For a moment, just try to live in these memories.

When you do this, your body is going to respond to the memory as though it is happening right now. You'll offer yourself the amnesty from fatigue without the need to change your current reality. The escape in your mind will remind you that it's possible to feel refreshed, and the effortless nature of recalling doesn't add any more to your plate.

Make decisions

Have you experienced the days when you were very fed up with every emotional weight you have been carrying that you have sworn to stop? You've told yourself you'd have enough. Just like someone who makes a New Year's resolution, in that moment of making decision and clarity, you felt an eruption of energetic pride, ready to deal with your new found resolution.

When you made this declaration, you made use of your thoughts to give yourself a burst of energy. With your clarity, you gained a higher state of energy. You might be telling yourself to stay forever, but by allowing yourself to be in that moment even just by thought and recognizing the relief you felt, you are able to push that feeling further and further every time, until it gains better drive.

Making a decision, using the power of your thinking to be deliberate in your life and takeover of the way you want to feel, gives a burst of energy you did not know was hidden within you. Most of our exhaustion comes from confusion and thinking that we are out of control. Simply making a decision, any decision regardless of how big or small it is will give you clarity that brings with it this life force of energy.

Vibrate higher

As an intuitive person, it's common to have high-highs and low-lows in terms of energy. While the connection we get way up there in vibration and with the snap of a finger, we can come crashing down.

The word for it is not really tired; I think the more appropriate word is depleted, emptied and drained of all motivation and energy. It is almost like our brains don't even want to think or do anything. Instead, we would just rather sit and be and not even have to talk to anyone sometimes. Like I said, completely depleted. Empathically and emotionally fatigued.

So, why are we exhausted all the time?

Intuitive people work in a different way than most in terms of using energy. We are persistently using and tapping into our energy reserves, even if we didn't mean to.

Whenever we feel the emotions of others, we're open to energy exchange. Empaths take on the energy of other people and release their energy to help others to heal. Mediums and those people who give readings use their energy in order to connect to Source and also to tap into another person's energy.

But this takes a lot of time and effort to work! We usually don't even feel or realize that we're doing it until it is too late!

I've recently noticed that today, I am either off or I'm on – nothing in between. I either get up and go or not move anywhere. This has been difficult for me since my wife NEVER stops being active unless she's asleep, and neither does my 5-year-old.

How Your Empath Gifts can lead to Adrenal Fatigue & Exhaustion?

It seems reasonable for empaths to experience a sudden onset of chronic fatigue because of a great crash of levels of energy.

This could be due to having different emotional responsibilities, and also for the reason that we copiously leak our energy when we don't remain present, grounded, consciously aware, and well-balanced.

Empaths usually feel drained when we have spent too much time around many people, and these interactions can make us develop emotional exhaustion. Empaths need a lot of alone time to relax and recharge their internal batteries.

Our feelings, thoughts, and emotions can all play chaos on our internal system, which causes disturbing consequences that can weaken us. If we have regular periods of solitude, we can process our feelings and emotions throughout the day. Then we will not become too exhausted, as we'll often let go of any negativity that might be going on our minds and weighing us down.

When we don't have the space to do this, we might find our minds are feverish at night when all things around us are still and quiet, and we're not distracted by external stimuli. This stops us from being able to relax in order for sleep to occur naturally.

We might also keep waking up throughout the night and not have a restful night's sleep, as our minds are always trying to process information and make sense of what happened throughout the day that is still lasting and has to be dealt with.

Our agitated minds lead to fatigue by unceasingly blasting us with a thunderous amount of stimuli, not letting us have the opportunity to rest, replenish, and recharge. This can lead to having unpredictable sleep patterns, some days needing 10 or more hours, while on the other days only one or two hours, depending on how much energy is attached to our energy field and pulling us down.

If we can't find time throughout the day to understand our internal thoughts, emotions, and feelings, it's essential to engage in meditation just before we go to sleep, in order for us to let our thoughts to blithely come and go without too much attention to them or kindling a hormone-induced physiological response.

Emotionally charged feelings linked to our memories and experiences can provoke us to feel emotions like anxiety, fear, panic, resentment, as well as paranoia – so our brains get convinced that we're under some kind of genuine threat. So, they deliver signals to our adrenal glands to create hormones, which then release a flow of energy.

When we experience penetrating or extended anxiety or stress, or our lifestyles are unhealthy – for example, we get too much of sleep or too little sleep, overworking, substance abuse, poor diet, stressful relationships, general life crises, or stressful family situations – we place too many continuous demands on our adrenal glands.

Our adrenal glands are little kidney-shaped endocrine glands, about the size of a walnut, that are located in the lower back area just above our kidneys. They're extremely powerful and beneficial to us when we are under stress, as they produce hormones that help keep us focused, alert, and increase our stamina so that we can deal with pressure.

The problem, however, is that when we over-stimulate our adrenal glands, they are going to keep generating energy, which can lead to a conflict when we're trying to sleep as we will feel enduringly wired and on high alert. This puts excessive stress on our adrenal glands, which makes them burn out and malfunction.

Managing Adrenal Fatigue

Adrenal fatigue roots from lower vibrational emotions. Every time we feel emotions that fall in a lower frequency, we start to feel like we're wading through mud. As empaths surrounded by a world full of people who are bored, stressed, lonely, sad, and fatigued themselves, we get immersed in lower rates, dragging us down consistently to the point that it feels normal.

When we're in these low levels of emotions, higher levels of emotions appear exhausting as we're seeing them from a place of no energy. We recognize that happiness, joy, and excitement comes from action and that action sounds impossible when we're feeling exhausted. But this view is tilted as it thinks that we are going to stay fatigued in those higher frequencies of emotions.

The truth is that as you work your way up the emotional scale, your energy goes up exponentially. So, how do you reach for higher levels of emotions when you feel so exhausted? One way to do that is to shift your thoughts ever so slightly to attain an emotion just higher than your current state.

Below are some tips you can follow to avoid experiencing adrenal fatigue.

1. Set Boundaries in Your Romantic Relationships

For many, dating is one of the best experiences in life – it feels like everything feels right in the world. This goes double for empaths. Those majestic butterflies in the stomach of an empath are multiplied as they're also feeling the butterflies in the stomach of their partner. It is a rare treat and one to be savored.

However, that deep connection made by the empath at the beginning of the relationship could be draining as times go by.

Even when your relationship is going well, feeling the emotions of your partner 24/7 is too much for anyone to handle. You may want to be with your partner at all times, but in order to keep your relationship on firm footing and your own emotional health intact, you have to make sure to take give yourself sometimes to breath – this could mean doing things alone and being on your own even just for once a week.

2. Be Yourself No Matter What Others Think

Being friends with an empath is truly a blessing. This means you have someone in your life that is fully aware of what you are feeling and thinking and can sometimes express it better than even you can.

Unfortunately for empaths, it's not rare to find people who don't appreciate their gifts. These are the same people who would say that you're "too sensitive" or even "overly dramatic." Due to who you are, you might feel like it's better to just put a load over your bright light just to make others feel more comfortable. Stop! Don't do it! You don't owe anything to anyone. If they can't accept you, then they don't deserve your loyalty. These people are toxic. Be yourself, and don't adjust only because they asked you to.

3. End Toxic Relationships

For an empath, relationships with people are vital. You love engaging in deep, meaningful conversations and exchanges of emotion. When a friend or a partner is in a critical situation, you shine as an advisor and shoulder to cry on.

But people who are always in the midst of a crisis can drain you dry and take advantage of your gift. You'll always feel obliged to help even the most distressed person you meet, but seek your own advice and when a relationship turns toxic, know that you are able to end it and no one will blame you for it.

4. Know the Culprit

Everyday exchanges can make or break an empath. Try to carry a journal with you and note down how the activities in your daily life make you feel.

Being an empath does not have to mean that doing yoga and meditation are the only things that can recharge you. Do anything else that makes you feel like you're in your comfort zone. It might be doing arts, cooking, playing video games, etc.

For everything that makes you feel invigorated, there is going to be something that will drain you — heavy traffic, deadlines, sudden change of weather, etc. The important thing is that you identify them and you do something to fix them.

5. Prioritize Time for Yourself

As an empath, a big part of your life is connecting with others. Being social is a big part of who you are as a person. That's the reason why you'll need to work hard in order to prioritize time for yourself. Have a "me" time every once in a while. You'll learn who's the more important thing in your life – you.

Probably an essential bit of advice I can give an empath is to feel everything. It is okay, no matter what other people say. You do you, so follow you.

Chapter 9

ADAPTING TO THE REAL WORLD

A few days ago, I had a conversation with someone about empathy. He said, "Sympathy is the most important thing in human communication, but sympathy without empathy doesn't have humanistic value. Someone may feel sympathy for you, but if he has no morals or feelings of empathy, he is able to use that sympathy against you."

This has me reflecting on empathy. To me, empathy is a process of feeling and understanding another person, as well as it's an internal reaction triggered by a cue from the other person.

The term empathy generally refers to two main concepts. The first concept involves the intellectual process of taking the psychological perspective of another person, imagining their feelings, thoughts, and what causes their actions and decisions. The second concept, which is usually a result of this perspective taking, is the feeling of an emotional reaction to the situation of another person.

Being empathetic – as an analytical method based on analogical thinking –might have its beginning in the very early days of the existence of any human beings, since toddlers start to learn empathy by imitating people that are around them. There's no way to measure, compare, observe, prove, or disprove that the specific emotion is experienced identically by different people. However, people may classify intensely with each other, and this identification may result in better understanding and emotional intimacy between individuals.

The truth is empathy is more important in social situations than it is psychologically. Despite the minor drawbacks of being an empathetic person, the existence of empathy may come as a great sign of self-awareness, healthy personal identity, self-worth, and in the positive sense, self-love. When empathy is lacking, a psychopathic or antisocial person can more easily exploit and abuse others.

9.1 How to Apply Empathy in Your Everyday Life

Aside from the fact that having greater empathy has great benefits for people around us, its effects are felt further by our immediate circle. There's no denying the fact that empathy can truly improve relationships, boost performance at work, and even benefit the environment significantly. Furthermore, it is really good for us. A lot of research has demonstrated that we're inherently social creatures by nature who have evolved to care for one another. Actually, you could say that lacking empathy goes against human nature.

Fortunately, empathy comes naturally to each one of us, which means that all we usually need is a gentle push in the right direction. So, to apply empathy in the real world, here are some practices you can follow.

6. Be curious

As children, we are all naturally nosy as we experience and see the world through fresh eyes. Unfortunately, as we become older, the monotony of routine may end up thudding this out of us. At the core of empathy is where a sense of curiosity is found – may it be to people, things, or situations. Whether it is your friend who looks anxious, the delivery man who brings you your letters, or the service crew at your local fast food, don't be afraid to ask a question about them.

7. Listen and comprehend

Be someone who actually listens and gives out total attention. Take the time to understand what a person is telling you and try to feel the emotion behind every word being said. A lot of the time when we're given the space to talk something through, we find the solution ourselves and a response is not even necessary.

8. Speak from your heart

Unfortunately, sometimes, being a good listener is not enough – again, empathy should not be a one-way street. In order to deepen a bond and truly make connections with others, we have to open up to another person and be ready to share our own weaknesses.

9. Face your prejudices

Whether we admit it or not, there have been times when we label people. Being empathetic has something to do with seeking harmonies, not differences. Volunteering offers a good way to push our boundaries and get in touch with people you would not otherwise meet in daily life.

10. Embrace the touchy-feely

When someone close to you decides to open up to you, don't be afraid to follow your instinct to reach out and give them a hug or at least a tap at the back! Research has suggested that physical contact improves levels of oxytocin, which improves the mood, lowers stress and blood pressure, and even speeds up the healing mechanisms of the body.

11. Practice loving-kindness meditation

So, how is this different from a simple meditation? Well, loving-kindness meditation means directing well-wishes to other people, may it be your close circle or strangers. Research has shown that practicing this on a regular basis does not only teach us how to improve kindness, but it also has deep effects on the part of the brain responsible for emotional intelligence and empathy.

9.2 How to Apply Empathy in Your Romantic Relationship

Empathy is necessary to nurture a relationship. In fact, without it, a relationship is set to fail. Here are some ways to improve understanding with your partner.

1. Be aware of the cues

A huge obstacle in feeling empathy toward our partners is getting stuck in our own perspective and power of feelings. When you find it hard to process the perspective of your partner, then pay attention to what you think is different on their body. Do they walk past as if they are avoiding you? Does their voice start to get louder? When you notice these, then there's probably something wrong. Don't be afraid to ask.

2. Give your genuine attention

When you're listening with full attention, you're doing great in understanding your partner. This also means that you are not focusing on your own response or planning a way to defend yourself as they talk.

3. Practice loving-kindness

Loving-kindness is the basis for the practice of mindfulness. It's free from judgment and invites clarity and calmness. The more we stay in touch with our foundation of loving-kindness, the easier it is for us to access empathy and be aware of our behavior and experience.

4. Look for the positive

Usually, partners get into the habit of concentrating on what's wrong with their partner, especially when they argue. This can surely get in the way of empathy. So, when you argue, instead of thinking of the negative things about your partner, start thinking of the positive reasons why you are in that relationship.

5. Be self-compassionate

Empathy starts with ourselves; it's hard to give out empathy to others if we neglect giving it to ourselves. That's why practicing self-compassion is very important. You heard that cliché that goes, "Learn to love yourself first before loving others"? Well, this is a good quote to live by. Always treat yourself with care, kindness, and understanding.

9.3 How to Apply Empathy at Workplace

While there might be times as though some of your colleagues entirely lack empathy, it's unlikely that they truly lack this most basic of human emotions. Showing empathy, however, is a different matter, and something a lot of people are struggling with, usually for fear of appearing weak or too emotional. Having emotional intelligence essential to building authoritative personal relationships by showing empathy at work is becoming vital. But by following the ideas listed below may help release the natural empathy traits you already have.

1. Always listen

When you're listening to someone, remind yourself that you're listening to understand, and not to answer. This small but significant difference means that you can fully concentrate on the person you are talking to, instead of feeling under pressure to make an appropriate response or answer. You can use active listening methods, considering your body language to show you are still following, as well as trying to summarize what you have heard and reflecting the actions and emotions of the individual you are speaking with.

Sounds simple, right? But this makes a vast difference. No matter what your level of interest is in the conversation, don't make them feel that you don't care. Showing disinterest is absolutely rude.

2. Be real

Unlike sympathy, empathy is something that cannot be faked or forced, which is both what makes it an authoritative leadership skill and what makes it complex to develop for some individual. Don't be afraid to open up about yourself for a little bit and to have meaningful relationships with your colleagues outside your work. Don't disregard or conceal the emotional content with a conversation with colleagues because this will feel like a fence to others. On the other hand, displaying some weakness and human feeling can potentially help relationships flourish.

Try to use appropriate physical contact – putting one of your hands on someone's back can mean a lot, and try to suitably see emotional signals in others. They are not obvious all the time, but make sure to pay attention if something is unusual in the mood or actions of your colleague. Ask them and make them feel that you are there for them if they want to open up, as long as they are comfortable.

3. Use all means of communication

When speaking to your team, always consider nonverbal communication, which could be as essential as the words you say. Research has shown that body language makes up, up to 93% of what others actually 'hear' in any form of communication.

Smile and make others do it as well. Not only will displaying positive body language be imitated by others and make relationships better, but it will also release endorphins, or what we called the happy hormones, which is responsible for making us feel better.

4. Avoid playing horns and halos

In recruiting, employers are taught to dwell on 'horns and halos,' which means the instant impression made by candidates that sometimes can appear as clear as soon as walked into the room – they are either wearing a horn or a halo. These first impressions are normally instigated by unconscious judgment and result from our subconscious looking for both similarities and differences in others and deducing that this is either a positive or a negative thing.

As much as possible, try not to judge others based on how they were the first time you encounter them and check your own prejudices where you see them. Real empathy has something to do with being able to walk in others' shoes.

Lastly, accept that it can be risky to show empathy. You need to put yourself 'out there' that, for many, can be something very scary. Lend your hands to others and be the one that makes the first move to initiate a connection and show support. It's a leap of faith that can be truly rewarding.

Conclusion

Empaths are superior, advanced souls that are incarnated on earth in growing numbers to bring light into the darkness during the time of sorrow. There are more empaths now than ever.

While every empath is a compassionate person, they are not all the same. For example, an emotional empath is someone who feels the emotional state of others. On the other hand, a physical empath can pick up on the physical ailments of others, usually feeling nauseated or getting headaches when someone around them is experiencing the same symptoms. I know someone who experiences muscle and joints pain and fatigue whenever she visits her grandfather, who has arthritis. On the other hand, a cognitive empath thinks about what others are feeling and why they are feeling it.

While most empaths are believed to be only either emotional or physical empaths, some of the empaths also feel the emotions of animals. These people can't stand being at the zoo. Global empaths can feel the emotions of humans all over the world, and watching the news is something that is very difficult for them. Other empaths are able to feel the energy of the earth and might even be able to foresee earthquakes and other calamities.

If you're an empath, you might have traits of one or several different types of an empath. And, no matter what type of empath you are, you might frequently feel exhausted or debilitated because of taking on pain of others.

www.ingramcontent.com/pod-product-compliance
Lightning Source LLC
Chambersburg PA
CBHW031115080526
44587CB00011B/976